THE MAISON
SAJOU
SEWING BOOK

THE MAISON

SAJOU

20 projects from the famous
French haberdashery

SEWING BOOK

LUCINDA GANDERTON

GIBBS SMITH
TO ENRICH AND INSPIRE HUMANKIND

Published by
Gibbs Smith
P.O. Box 667
Layton, Utah 84041
1.800.835.4993 orders
www.gibbs-smith.com

This book was conceived, designed, and produced by **Ivy Press**
210 High Street, Lewes, East Sussex, BN7 2NS, U.K.

CREATIVE DIRECTOR Peter Bridgewater
PUBLISHER Susan Kelly
COMMISSIONING EDITOR Sophie Collins
ART DIRECTOR Wayne Blades
SENIOR EDITORS Jacqui Sayers & Jayne Ansell
DESIGNER Kevin Knight
COPY-EDITOR Sarah Hoggett
PHOTOGRAPHER Neal Grundy
STYLIST Hélène Adamczewski
ILLUSTRATOR Cathy Brear

Printed and bound in China
Color origination by Ivy Press Reprographics

ISBN: 978-1-4236-3490-4
Library of Congress Control Number: 2013948625

Contents

Introduction *The Sajou Sewing Book*

FOR MANY YEARS A BYWORD for pretty and refined French taste, the esteemed Maison Sajou supplies the world's most discerning needleworkers with their linen and embroidery thread, as well as with a covetable selection of sewing equipment that includes pearl-handled scissors and silver thimbles. This book brings that sophisticated sensibility to twenty desirable projects that you can create for yourself, your home, and your family. Table linen, cushions, and a tote bag, along with smaller but equally gorgeous accessories, such as a velvet clutch bag and a flower-strewn gadget case, all acquire French style with simple but lovely embroidery.

From the earliest planning stages, I wanted these projects to reflect Sajou's rich heritage and, although they incorporate traditional techniques, they have all been designed with a fresh twist to suit contemporary lives and interiors. My own favorites are the sampler cushion on page 126, derived from classic alphabet charts in Frédérique Crestin-Billet's personal archive, and the charcoal gray border pattern on the sophisticated lampshade on page 104, which is based on a piece of antique lace. The scrapbook-style "mood boards" show some of my other diverse sources of inspiration: striped ticking, Marie Antoinette's slippers, Versailles' royal vegetable garden, butterflies, and dandelion clocks.

There is something here for every level of ability, from classic cross-stitch monograms for the complete novice to all-but-forgotten (but easily learned) techniques, such as drawn threadwork for the more experienced stitcher. The straightforward step sequences provide illustrated guidance throughout, and in the following reference section, I've covered all the basic sewing skills you will need, along with details and diagrams showing how to work the embroidery stitches. I hope that you will have as much pleasure in reading this book as I have derived from writing it.

Lucinda Ganderton

Techniques

longues – du n° 3 au n° 9

SAJOU

15 aiguilles à coudre assorties

Basic sewing kit

Each of our projects starts with a "you will need" list, which details all the sewing accessories and materials required. The last, but most important, item is "basic sewing kit": the tools and equipment required for all basic stitching tasks. You may already have most of these in your workbox, but here's an overview of essential equipment.

Needles

Although they all look similar, there are several different types of needles, each designed for a special purpose. They come in different lengths and widths, from no. 1 to no. 12. The higher the number, the thinner and shorter the needle. The length is a matter of personal preference, but if a needle is too thin for the thread you are using, you will find that it won't slip easily through the fabric. Always keep your needles in the original package or a needle book because they tend to disappear into the filling of pincushions.

• **Sharps** are medium length and have oval eyes. They are the most commonly used needles, ideal for hand sewing, tacking, and other general stitching.
• **Embroidery or crewel needles** are similar to sharps, but have long eyes that accommodate several strands of thread.
• **Tapestry needles** have blunt tips that slip easily between the threads of embroidery linen and needlepoint canvas. They come in many sizes, intended for two strands of embroidery cotton up to knitting yarn.

• **Quilting or between needles** are short and fine with a round eye for a single length of sewing thread. Use these for appliqué, quilting, and detailed hand sewing.

Pins

Slender straight pins are made
from rustproof steel and have tiny
silver tops. Pins with round glass
tops look prettier, are easier to
handle, and show up well against
fabric. Store your pins in a small
container or transfer them to a
pincushion. A small magnet is useful
for rounding up strays, and a few
safety pins will come in handy.

Thimble

Almost everybody's grandmother
wore her thimble when sewing,
but they are not so commonly used
today. If you intend to do a lot of
hand work, a thimble will prevent
your finger from becoming sore
and punctured.

Scissors

A well-stocked sewing box should
have at least three pairs of scissors,
each kept for its own particular
task. Good scissors will last for
many years, so it is worth investing
in the best-quality steel blades.
• **Embroidery scissors** are small
with short, pointed blades and
sharp tips. They are necessary for
snipping threads and trimming
knots. Seam rippers are also useful
for removing thread and unpicking.
• **Medium general-purpose
scissors** are used for cutting out
smaller fabric shapes and all of
your paper patterns.
• **Large tailor's shears** have
angled handles and should be
reserved for cutting only cloth,
because paper will blunt the blades.

Measuring up

Tape measures are invaluable. You will need an accurate long cloth measure for large-scale projects. A small ruler is useful for checking hem turnings. Large sheets of dressmaker's pattern paper, which are printed with an allover grid, will save time when making square and rectangular templates.

Embroidery hoops

These lightweight frames come in several sizes, from 5 to 12 inches (12.5 to 30 cm) in diameter. They consist of two wooden rings that hold the fabric taut. The inner ring is a complete circle and the outer one is split, with a metal screw attached to the outside edge so that it can be tightened.

Marking out

Fadeaway, air-erasable marking pens—felt-tips with a pigment that disappears after a few days—are ideal for transferring templates, marking button positions, or for drawing freehand onto fabric. If you are not going to complete your project immediately, it may be wiser to use a chalk pencil or a sharp pencil instead. Dressmaker's carbon paper is a good alternative for marking accurate outlines.

Sewing machine

There is a huge range of sewing machines available, many of which are capable of advanced techniques. However, the projects in this book require only straight seaming, so all you will need is a basic model. Read the manual carefully and remember that, as with hand sewing, you will need a package of assorted needles for different fabrics.

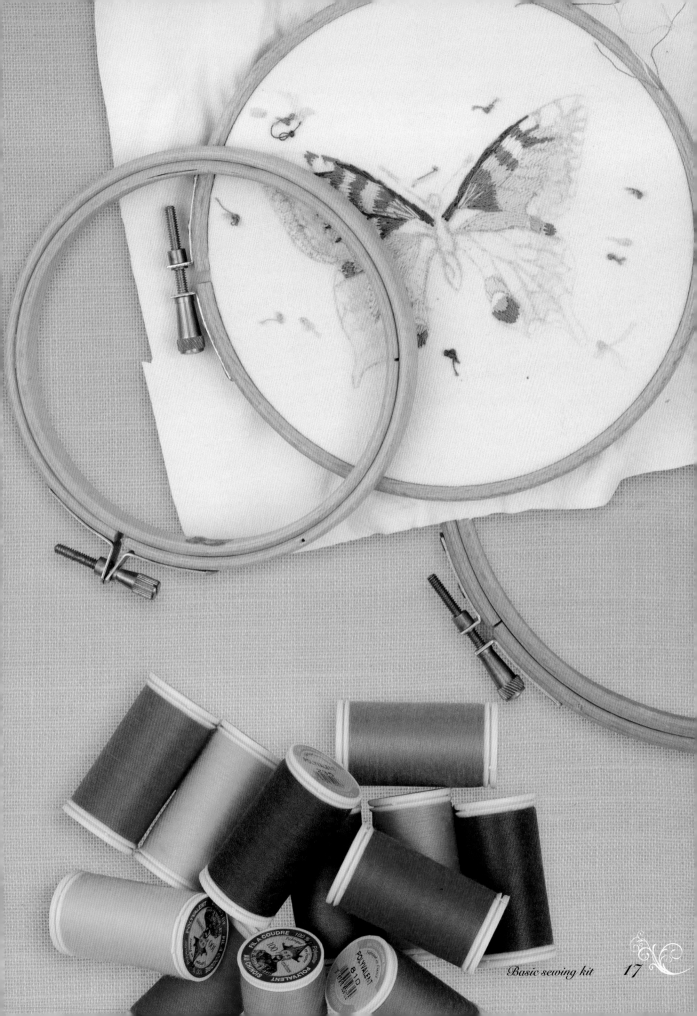

Materials

The "you will need" section of each project gives details of the threads, fabrics, ribbons, buttons, and trimmings we used, along with their colors. You can re-create the items exactly as we made them, or reinterpret them in a plan to suit your own taste and interior.

Embroidery thread

• **Stranded cotton** is made up of several loosely twisted strands that can be easily separated, depending on the size of stitch required. Sajou Retors du Nord, which has four strands, comes on cards of almost 22 yards (20 m) in nearly 100 colors. Other manufacturers produce skeins of six-stranded thread. If you are using one of these threads, always work a sample first; the thickness of the threads and, therefore, the stitch size and shape may vary.

• **Metallic thread**, such as our Tonkin thread, used for special effects, incorporates fine, flexible metallic strands that add a touch of glitter to your stitches.

• **Stranded wool** varies between manufacturers. Sajou's Laine Saint-Pierre, a fine stranded wool, originally intended for darning, comes in many subtle shades. Other crewel wools tend to be slightly thicker, so check

the number of strands you need before starting.

• **Thread cards** are both useful and decorative. You can wind your odd lengths of thread around them for future use so that nothing is wasted.

Remember that embroidered items, including table linen, should only be laundered by hand in warm water, because the colors may run and the stitches may be ruined in a high-temperature machine wash.

Sewing threads

All-purpose cotton-wrapped polyester threads are suitable for all fabrics, but natural cotton thread has a fine luster and is good for seams on cotton materials. Use a contrasting color when basting or tacking, so that you can easily see and remove the large stitches.

Embroidery fabric

You can sew onto almost any type of cloth, but there is a whole range of fabrics that have been designed for hand stitching, categorized by the width of the individual threads. Sajou embroidery linen, which comes in 27 colors, has 32 threads per inch (12 threads per cm), which makes it ideal for fine cross-stitch and free embroidery. Other evenweave fabrics include stiff Aida cloth, which has a mesh of squares and is good for beginners, because no individual thread counting is involved. Needlepoint canvas has a more open grid for thicker woollen stitches.

Trims

It's the fine details that make a needlework project really stand out, so take time choosing the perfect trimmings. A whole wealth of ribbons, from household name tapes to floral braids woven on antique looms, is available from Sajou and other manufacturers. Edging lace, including guipure and imitation bobbin lace, has one straight side that can be stitched along hems; insertion lace has two straight edges and, as its name suggests, is inserted between two pieces of fabric. Cheerful rickrack has a zigzag appearance. Bias binding, available in several widths, is used to neaten seams and thick fabric edges. Buttons are practical closures, but also add little bursts of color to your embroidery.

Practical fabrics

These are the unglamorous but essential materials that give your projects a professional look.
• **Interfacing** is a firm fabric that is inserted between two layers of fabric to stiffen a bag or garment. It can be basted or tacked in. Different weights are available, depending on the firmness required.
• **Fusible interfacing** is an iron-on interfacing with a heat-sensitive layer that bonds it firmly in place. You can use it for ironing on appliqué motifs, and it is also useful if you need to sandwich together two layers to make a stiff fabric.
• **Batting** comes in natural or synthetic fibers and is used in quilt making to give a soft, padded look.

Cottons & linens

Simple striped cottons provide ample scope for embellishment, while patterned cottons, such as Sajou's own collections, Liberty Tana Lawn, and other dressmaking fabrics, make interesting backings, borders, and linings. Heavy vintage sheeting has a softness that only comes from long use, and can be reused for napkins and tablecloths. Be sure to first launder it well and discard any worn areas.

Sewing techniques

The illustrated step-by-step instructions for each of the projects show you exactly how to prepare, embroider, and then stitch together the various items. The basic sewing techniques involved may already be familiar, but the explanations below will help the novice and serve as a reminder to the more experienced needleworker.

Preparing the fabric

If you are making an item that will be laundered at some stage, it is wise to wash and iron the fabric before you start to allow for shrinkage. Special 32-count embroidery linen, however, should not be washed, or it will lose its shape. Press all fabrics well before cutting out to remove any creases; a light spray of starch should remove stubborn fold marks.

Portable pencil holder
page 58

Making patterns & cutting out

Most of the projects are made from simple squares or rectangles of fabric, and measurements are given. Mark these figures onto squared dressmaker's paper and cut along the printed lines to make your pattern pieces. Pin them onto the fabric with the edges aligning with the grain (threads), and cut along the edges with long scissors.

Bordered bolster
page 110

Alternatively, you can cut out the shapes directly using a clear plastic quilter's ruler, a cutting mat, and a rotary cutter. Use a pair of compasses for circles, like those at the ends of the Bordered bolster on page 110. Smaller shapes are given as full-size templates that you can trace or photocopy.

Hems & binding

A raw edge can be finished off in two ways: by folding it back and securing it down, or by covering it with a strip of fabric or bias binding. This method is used for thicker fabrics and for neatening double layers of fabric, as on the Portable pencil holder (see page 58).

A single hem has just a single turning and is used when the back of the fabric is hidden. A double hem is folded over twice to create a firm, reversible edge for table or bed linen. The depth of the turnings is always given in the instructions.

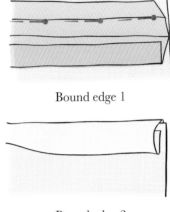

Bound edge 1

Bound edge 2

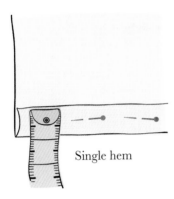

Single hem

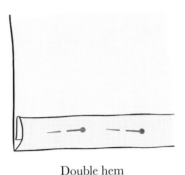

Double hem

Single hem

With the right side of the fabric facing downward, turn back the edge to the required depth. Use a tape measure or a ruler to make sure that the turning is consistent all the way along, then press, baste, or pin as directed.

Double hem

Fold and press the first turning as for a single hem, then fold back the edge once again, to the depth given. Pin, then machine stitch $^1/_8$ inch (3 mm) from the inner fold, or slip-stitch along the folded edge (see page 23) by hand.

Bound edge

1 Open out one edge of the bias binding, or bias tape. With the right sides together, pin it along the edge of the fabric, then machine stitch along the first fold.
2 Turn the fabric over and fold the binding to the right side to enclose the raw edges. Baste down and machine stitch close to the fold. You can also slip-stitch the folded edge by hand for a less obtrusive finish.

Bound corners

1 Baste the binding down as above, until the distance from the corner is the same as the depth of the first turning— usually about $^1/_4$ inch (5 mm). Fold the tape across to the right at a 45-degree angle and press. Now fold it back to the left, along the edge of the fabric, and continue basting near the fold. Machine stitch along the fold.
2 Finish off by turning the binding to the back and refold the creases. Baste under the surplus to make a neatly mitered corner.

Bound corners 1

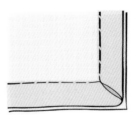

Bound corners 2

Straight seam

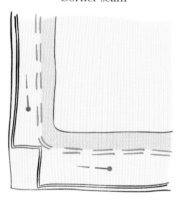

Corner seam

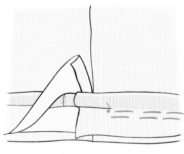

Piped seam 1

Seams

The "seam allowance" is the distance between the edge of the fabric and the stitch line. The footplate of your machine is engraved with a series of straight lines; pick the one marked with the required measurement and keep the edge of the fabric parallel with it as you stitch. When the seam is finished, press the seam allowance to one side, or open, as instructed. The seam allowance on corner seams—on bags, for example—needs to be trimmed before the work is turned right side out.

Straight seam

With right sides together, pin the two edges together. Machine stitch along the given seam allowance. Reinforce both ends of the seam by working a few reverse stitches.

Corner seam

Sew along the first edge as far as the end of the seam allowance. Keeping the needle down, lift up the presser foot and turn the fabric 90 degrees. Lower the foot and continue along the second edge. Trim a small triangle from the seam allowance to reduce the bulk and make sure that the seam will lie flat. Turn right side out and ease out the corner with a knitting needle or blunt pencil, then press.

Piping

Piping—a soft cotton cord covered with a narrow bias-cut strip of fabric—gives a professional, upholstered finish to any soft-furnishing project.

To make your own bias binding for piping, mark a diagonal line across a square of fabric, from corner to corner. Draw a series of lines parallel to it and 1½ inches (4 cm) apart, then cut along them. Join the short ends of the strips as necessary, pressing the seam allowances open, until you have the required length.

Piped seams

With the right side (if there is one) of the fabric facing outward, fold this bias binding strip around the piping cord and baste in place ⅛ inch (3 mm) from the piping cord itself.

1 Pin and baste the piping to the right side of the first piece of fabric, lining up the raw edges. Clip into the seam allowance on the fabric strip when you reach a corner, to within ⅛ inch (3mm) of the basting. This will allow you to turn the piping cord around the corner of the fabric neatly.

2 To keep the seam in a round of piping inconspicuous, position it next to a seam or at the center bottom edge. Baste the piping in place, leaving a 1-inch (2.5-cm) overlap on each side of the seam. Unpick just over 1 inch (3 cm) of basting stitches at each end of the piping and trim the cord so that the ends butt up together. Stitch them loosely together. Fold one end of the strip under the other to create a neat join. Baste both ends together.

Piped seam 2

3 Pin and baste the second piece of fabric to the first, with right sides facing. Using a zipper foot and thread to match the piping, machine stitch all the way around the piping, as close to the cord as possible.

Zippers

A zipper gives a neat and practical finish for a cushion cover.

To insert a zipper in a flat seam, pin and baste the two sides together along the seam allowance, then machine stitch each end, leaving a gap in the center that is $\frac{5}{8}$ inch (1.5 cm) longer than the zipper. Reinforce both ends of the seams. Press the seam allowance open. Baste the open zipper in place on the wrong side of the opening.

Fit a zipper foot to your machine and, with the right side facing upward, sew along one edge of the fabric, from top to bottom, about $\frac{1}{8}$ inch (4 mm) from the teeth. Just before you reach the zipper pull, raise the presser foot, keeping the needle down. Gently slide the pull behind the needle. Lower the foot and continue stitching to the end. Close the zipper again. Sew across the end, just outside the metal tab across the teeth, then stitch the other side as before. Finish off by sewing across the top end, just outside the second tab.

Hand sewing

Most of the seaming and hemming in this book is done by machine, but there are two hand stitches that you should be familiar with.

Basting (or tacking)
This is a longer version of running stitch (see page 28), used to hold two pieces of fabric together temporarily before machine stitching a seam. Keep the stitches and the spaces between them the same length— between $\frac{1}{4}$ and $\frac{3}{8}$ inch (6 and 10 mm). Use a contrasting color thread so it is easier to see and unpick the stitches when the seam is finished.

Slip stitch
Use this to create an unobtrusive seam between two pieces of fabric. Bring the needle up just below the edge of the lower piece and insert it directly above in the other fabric. Come out again, $\frac{1}{4}$ inch (6 mm) to the left. Make a small downward stitch into the first fabric and continue to the end.

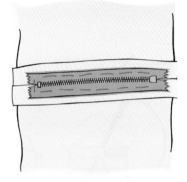

Zipper

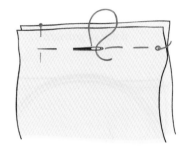

Basting

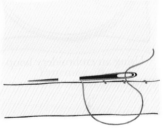

Slip stitch

Cross-stitch

Cross-stitch is a traditional technique that has long been used for embroidering samplers, alphabets, and monograms. Vary the size of the stitches by altering the number of threads worked over.

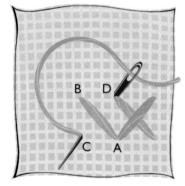

Single stitches 1

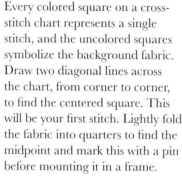

Single stitches 2

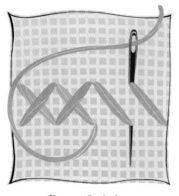

Rows of stitches

Following a chart

Every colored square on a cross-stitch chart represents a single stitch, and the uncolored squares symbolize the background fabric. Draw two diagonal lines across the chart, from corner to corner, to find the centered square. This will be your first stitch. Lightly fold the fabric into quarters to find the midpoint and mark this with a pin before mounting it in a frame.

Working the stitches

Each square cross-stitch is made up of two diagonal stitches that are worked over the same number of threads in each direction. You can work the stitches one at a time, or in rows made up of sloping stitches lying in opposite directions. If you are using a shaded thread, always work single crosses, or the subtle coloring will be lost.

Single stitches
1 Bring the needle up at A and down diagonally to the left at B, taking it over the specified number of threads. Come up again at C, level with A and directly below B.
2 Insert the needle at D, directly above A, to complete the second slanting stitch, then bring it out at C, ready for the next cross.

Rows of stitches
Work the first line of diagonal stitches from right to left, then stitch the second line across them in the opposite direction. You can build up larger blocks of stitches in rows like this.

Half cross-stitch
This useful filler stitch is, as the name suggests, just half of a cross-stitch. A single diagonal line, it is represented on cross-stitch charts as a half triangle. The diagonal side of the triangle shows you the direction in which the stitch should slope.

Needlepoint

A needlepoint project has to be pinned onto a small rectangular "stretcher" frame. Each square on the needlepoint chart stands for a single stitch, in this case a tent stitch. A block of sixteen small squares represents the seven diagonal stitches that make up a Scotch stitch. Start and finish each thread as for the embroidery stitches.

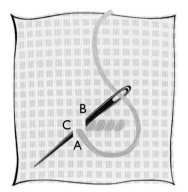

Tent stitch 1

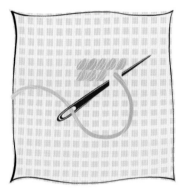

Tent stitch 2

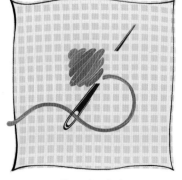

Scotch stitch

Tent stitch

1 This neat diagonal stitch is worked over the intersection of two single threads. Make a small diagonal stitch from A up to B and bring the needle out level with A, at C, to start the next one. Continue to the end of the row.
2 Work the next row in the opposite direction, from left to right. Continue working alternately from right to left and left to right to fill the space.

Scotch stitch

Start each Scotch stitch at the top left corner with a tent stitch, then work three increasingly longer stitches in the same direction, over two, three, and then four thread intersections. Complete the square by reducing the length of the next three stitches. Start the next stitch at the top right corner, one intersection along, and repeat the seven stitches.

Blocking

The diagonal nature of the stitches means that the canvas tends to distort, but this can be put right by "blocking" it. Cut out a piece of paper the same size as the finished item. Tape it to a board and cover with a clear plastic bag. Spray the canvas lightly with water. With the right side facing downward, use thumbtacks to pin the top edge so that the stitches are in line with the template. Stretch the canvas so the bottom edge is aligned with the template, then do the same along the other two sides. Add more thumbtacks at $3/4$-inch (2-cm) intervals and let dry.

Outline & border stitches

The stitches in this group are all worked continuously to create straight and curved lines, or to "draw" a shape onto fabric, following the template outline. Use a single strand of thread for a delicate line, or up to four for a stronger, darker look.

Running stitch

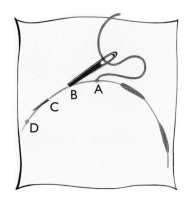

This is simply a row of short straight stitches, all the same length and spaced equally apart. The first stitch that most beginners learn, it is used to baste or hand seam two pieces of fabric together, as well as for quilting. Running stitch is useful for embroidering flexible outlines, such as the "squiggles" on the Portable pencil holder (see page 58).

1 Bring the needle up at A, then take it down at B to make the first stitch.
2 Come up again at C and down at D so that the second stitch is the same length as the one you have just made.
3 Continue along the line, making sure that the spaces between the stitches are equal.

Whipped running stitch

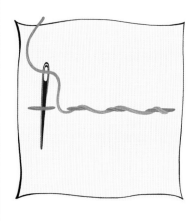

Also known as cordonnet stitch, this is an embellished version of running stitch. It can be worked with two contrasting threads to give a pretty candy-cane effect or in a single color for a fine twisting line—for example, the roots and tendrils on the Vegetable napkins (see page 38). Use a tapestry needle for the lacing to avoid piercing the fabric or thread.

1 Start with a foundation row of running stitches, spacing them closer together than usual.
2 Bring the second thread up halfway along the first stitch, and slip the needle under the second stitch from top to bottom.
3 Do the same at the third stitch, then carry on "whipping" each stitch to the end of the row.

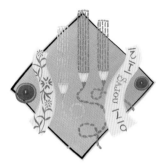

Portable pencil holder
page 58

Vegetable napkins
page 38

Picture sewing tidy
page 80

Backstitch

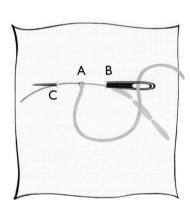

This creates a plain, unbroken line that is useful for illustrative outlines, such as the scissors and cotton reels on the Picture sewing tidy (see page 80). It is also used to define shapes that will subsequently be filled in, such as raised satin stitch. As its name suggests, the stitches are worked in the opposite way to the progression of the line.

1 Start at point A and take the needle backward to B to make the first stitch.
2 Following the guide line, come out again at C, one stitch length ahead of A.
3 Pull the needle through and take it backward, inserting it at A. Continue working backstitches of equal length, all the way to the end of the line.

Stem stitch

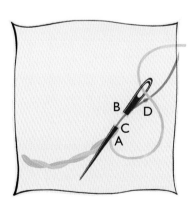

The name of this stitch reveals its traditional use: embroidering flower stems. It is perfect for any flexible outlines, so we chose it for the sinuous stems of the lavender sprigs on page 62. Follow the guideline carefully, and always keep the thread to the right of the needle. Check the wrong side of the fabric when you've finished—you'll see a row of backstitch.

1 This stitch is worked from left to right. Bring the needle up at A and insert it again at B, making a long stitch.
2 Come up at point C, halfway between A and B.
3 Take the needle down at D, making a stitch the same length as A-B. Bring it up again at B. Repeat along the row, working a line of overlapping stitches.

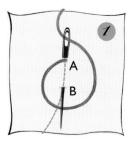
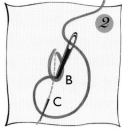
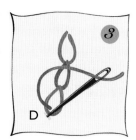

Summer tote bag
page 46

Chain stitch

This is the first of the looped outline stitches, in which the thread is passed under the needle. Make sure that all the stitches are the same length and try not to pull the thread up too tightly, so that each link in the chain is rounded. The wide line that it creates is good for letters and strong outlines that need to stand out against their

background, such as the motifs on the Summer tote bag (see page 46).
1 Bring the needle up at A, the start of the line. Loop the thread from left to right and insert the needle at the same point where it emerged, at A. Following the guideline, bring the point up again at B so that it passes above the thread.

2 Draw the needle through and over the thread to make the first loop. Take it back through the fabric at B, looping the thread as before. Bring the tip up at C.
3 Repeat this all the way along the line. Anchor the last loop at D, with a small straight stitch.

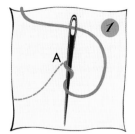
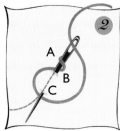
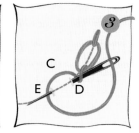

Cable chain stitch

The technique for this is a little more complicated, but it's worth the effort because it is an interesting stitch. It is good for curved and straight lines, and its graphic appearance made it perfect for the anchor chains on the Summer tote bag (see page 46). It works best with several strands of thread, so that the individual links stand out clearly.

1 Bring the needle up at point A. Wrap the thread over and then under the tip, from right to left.
2 Take the needle down at B, just a short distance along the line from A. Loop the thread from left to right, as for chain stitch, and bring the needle out again at C, over the thread.

3 Gently pull the needle through to form a straight stitch and a chain stitch. Wrap the thread around the needle as in step 1 and then work the next loop from D to E. Carry on stitching in this way to the end of the line, and anchor the final link with a straight stitch as for chain stitch.

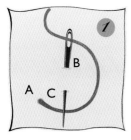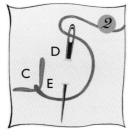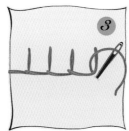

Blanket stitch

Originally used for tidying the edges of woollen blankets, this versatile stitch can be used to add a decorative edge to any nonfraying fabric and for joining two pieces together. It also makes a good embroidery stitch that is useful for outlining circles or concealing the raw edge of an appliqué motif.

1 Start at A, the beginning of the line you will be stitching along, or at the edge of the fabric. Take the needle up to the right and insert it at B. Come out again, directly below, at C, so that the tip is above the looped thread.

2 Pull the needle through, over the thread, and make the next stitch from D to E. Repeat this step to continue along the line, keeping the stitches the same height and equidistant.
3 Finish off by making a small straight stitch over the final loop.

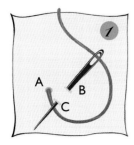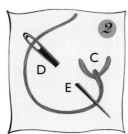

Silk slipper bag
page 96

Feather stitch

This pretty stitch was used to embellish nineteenth-century lingerie and English countrymen's smocks. It can be worked in straight or curved lines and has a coral-like appearance. Like blanket stitch, it is used to conceal seam lines in appliqué and it works well in combination with other stitches; we added contrasting French knots

to make a striking border on the Silk slipper bag (see page 96).
1 Come up at A and insert the needle across to the right, at B. Bring the tip out centered below, at C. Pull through over the thread.

2 Work the next stitch to the left. Take the needle down at D, in line with C and bring it out at E.
3 Continue making stitches to the right and left and fasten down the final loop with a small straight stitch.

Filling stitches

The four stitches here are worked within a marked shape, in much the same way that you would fill in an outline with paint. All of them give a solid block of color and each has its own look and application. The step-by-step instructions for the projects tell you which to use, but it's useful to know how to embroider them all.

Satin stitch

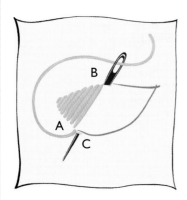

This is simply a series of parallel straight stitches, all worked at the same angle and spaced so closely together that they produce a smooth and lustrous surface. If you are filling in a leaf or petal, position the stitches in the same direction as the outline. For more geometric shapes, such as squares or narrow borders, set them at right angles to the outside edge.

Bring the needle up at A and make a straight stitch across to B. Start the next stitch close to A, at C, then continue until the shape is filled in.

Raised satin stitch

Choose a raised variation to give your embroidered shapes a padded, sharply defined edge. There are two ways of doing this: as shown here, or by first filling in the shape loosely with straight stitches and working satin stitch at an angle over this foundation. You can see this technique on the Dandelion crib sheet (see page 66).

Outline the motif with a round of small backstitches, then work satin stitch over this foundation so that the outside edge will be raised slightly above the fabric.

Dandelion crib sheet
page 66

Vegetable napkins
page 38

Butterfly collection
page 72

Encroaching satin stitch

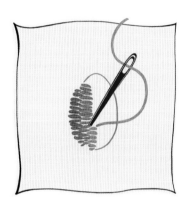

Use this stitch when you need to blend different colors to produce a shaded, three-dimensional effect. For a subtle change of color, pick out two or more closely related threads. For more contrast, choose contrasting light and dark threads. We used this stitch for the Vegetable napkins on page 38.

Work along the left edge of the shape with satin stitch in the first shade and change the color as necessary. For each stitch in the following rows, bring the needle out at the right and insert it between two stitches on the previous row so that the colors overlap slightly.

Straight stitch

Straight stitch filling is used to "color in" irregular shapes and gives a more random look than the regular finish of satin stitch. You can see the painterly effect that this gives on the Butterfly collection (see page 72), where each of the centered blue stitches is worked at a slightly different angle.

Think of each stitch as an individual brushstroke, varying their length and direction as you fill in each area of the motif.

Isolated stitches

These individual stitches are often used singly as accents, to create highlights of color within a design. They can also be repeated to create texture and pattern, arranged either in regular rows or on a geometric grid, or scattered randomly like the seeds on the Dandelion crib sheet on page 66.

French knot

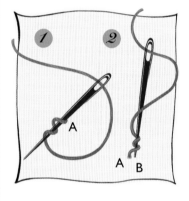

These round, three-dimensional knots are good for adding small bursts of color to any embroidery. They can also be worked closely together to make a more solid shape. The centers of the daisies on the Daisy-dot gadget case on page 90 consist of small circles of tightly packed French knots.

1 Bring the needle through the fabric at A. Holding the thread taut, wrap it twice around the tip of the needle, then draw the loops up by pulling gently on the thread.
2 Keeping the tension, reinsert the needle close to A, at B, and push it down through the loops so that the thread forms a small round knot.

Star stitch

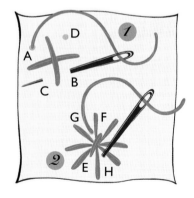

1 Start with an upright cross-stitch, then sew a diagonal cross directly over it, from A to B and C to D.
2 Now work a small elongated cross to anchor these stitches, from E to F and G to H. This creates a raised effect at the center of the stitch.

Country kitchen tray cloth
page 138

Lazy daisy stitch

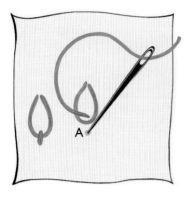

Each lazy daisy stitch is an anchored loop, like a single link of chain stitch. They make naturalistic petals and leaves and were the perfect choice for the flower heads on the Provençal tablecloth (see page 62).

1 Make a single link, as in step 1 of chain stitch (see page 30), then jump straight to step 3 and make a short straight stitch to A, anchoring the loop.

Stamen stitch

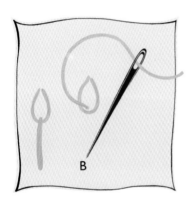

1 Extend the straight stitch of lazy daisy, above, to point B and you have a stamen stitch. These are used as the stems of the dandelion seed heads on the Dandelion crib sheet (see page 66).

Dandelion crib sheet
page 66

Fly stitch

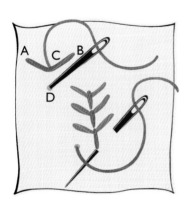

This small v-shape stitch is made up of a loose straight stitch and a small straight stitch that anchors it down in the same way as a lazy daisy stitch. It can be worked singly, as we used it for the seagulls on the Summer tote bag (see page 46), or in rows as a wide outline stitch.

1 Bring the needle up at A and take it down at B to make a straight stitch, but don't pull it through completely. Come up again at C, equidistant from A and B, and above the thread, then pull up the thread. Take it down again at D to complete the anchor stitch.

The Projects

Vegetable napkins

.... *with finely embroidered motifs*

The perfect accompaniment to a summer salad or a warm winter soup, these four embroidered vegetables will enliven any meal time. Instructions for making the actual napkins are given within the project, but you can easily update an existing set or use already-made linen, if you prefer. The motifs could also be used singly or together around the kitchen to decorate an apron, dish towel, or recipe book cover. If you have the time and dedication, there's always the possibility of completing the table setting with a matching runner or cloth.

Finished size
....

18 inches (46 cm) square

You will need

* **Four 20-inch (50-cm) squares of laundered white or cream linen**

* **Colored thread** for basting

* **Sewing thread** to match fabric

* **Templates** on page 163

* **Stranded embroidery thread** in seven colors: orange, light green, olive green, pale orange, red, ivory, and yellow-green (we used Maison Sajou Retors du Nord in 2405 orange; 2013 fern; 2445 olive; 2540 mandarin; 2032 red; 2196 ivory; and 2449 nile)

* **Basic sewing kit** (see pages 14–16)

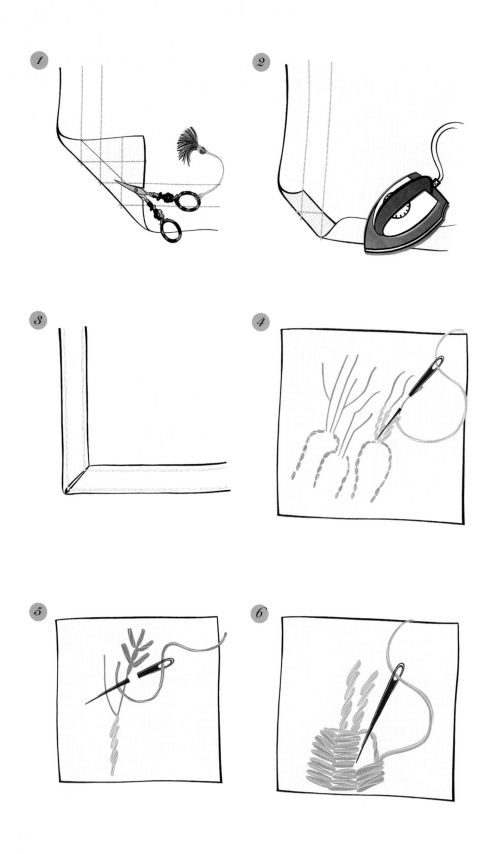

The Projects

Making the napkins

The napkins are finished with a double hem. Turn under ½ inch (12 mm) along each edge of each linen square and press, then press under a second turning, also of ½ inch (12 mm). Unfold both creases.

1

The surplus fabric now has to be trimmed and pressed to create mitered (or 45-degree) corners. Turn back the corner to form a right angle, carefully matching the crease lines. Press the folded edge lightly. Snip off the tip of the triangle, along the diagonal shown.

2

Refold and repress the original creases to create a neat right angle at the corner.

3

Neaten the other three corners in the same way, then baste down the turnings. Secure the hem with two rounds of machine stitching, working the first one ⅛ inch (3 mm) from the inner fold and the second one ⅛ inch (3 mm) from the outside edge. Remove the basting stitches.

Embroidering the motifs

Following the instructions on page 24, trace or photocopy the templates on page 163 and transfer one motif to a corner of each napkin. Position them about 2 inches (5 cm) in from each side of the corner. Embroider the motifs as instructed below, using two strands of thread throughout; you can find details of how to work all the stitches on pages 28–35.

Carrots

4

Stitch over the outline of the carrots with small backstitches, using orange thread. Work stem stitch in light green thread over the lower part of the leaf stems.

5

Embroider the leaf fronds in olive green thread, working one small vertical stitch at the top of each guide line, then a line of four to seven fly stitches below it.

6

Fill in the carrots with encroaching satin stitch, extending the stitches over the backstitch outlines to give depth to the motifs. Use one strand of pale orange and one of orange for the left carrot, two strands of orange for the center one, and two of pale orange for the carrot on the right.

Finish off by adding a few straight stitches in olive green along the sides of the carrots.

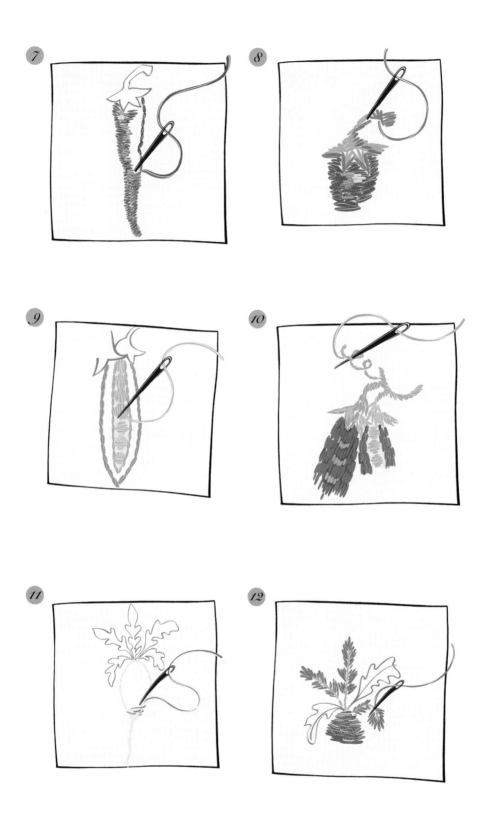

Chili peppers

7

Outline the peppers in backstitch as for the carrots, using red thread. Embroider the long highlights with orange satin stitch and the rectangular highlights with ivory satin stitch. Fill in the rest of the chili pepper with encroaching satin stitch in red.

8

Embroider the hull and stem in olive green satin stitch, altering the angle of the stitches to follow the direction of the outline. Work the shadowed areas along the side of the stem and the points of the hull in light green satin stitches.

Pea pods

9

Backstitch around the outside of the left pod and the inner and outer lines of the left pod with two strands of light green thread. Using yellow-green thread, embroider vertical satin stitches over each of the peas to act as padding, then work horizontal stitches on top. Fill in the triangular spaces with small ivory straight stitches.

Fill in the rest of the pod with encroaching satin stitch worked vertically in light green thread. Work extra stitches down the middle on each side in olive green to add highlights.

Embroider the crescents on the left pod with olive green satin stitch, worked vertically. Fill in the pod with encroaching satin stitch in light green thread, working over the backstitch outline.

10

Work the hulls and stems as for the chili peppers, in light green and olive green thread, then embroider the tendril in small whipped backstitches in olive green. "Whip" by passing the needle under the stitches, as for whipped running stitch (see page 28).

Radish

11

Use two strands of ivory thread to backstitch over the outline of the radish, then fill it in with encroaching satin stitch. The blended-color effect is created by using one strand of ivory and one of red together for the light areas and two strands of red for the darker parts. The plain color root and lower part are worked with two strands of ivory.

12

Work the second, third, and fifth leaves in light green satin stitch, angling the stitches to match the outline. Sew a line of small olive green backstitches down the center of each leaf. Stitch the first and fourth leaves in olive green thread with light green center lines.

The Potager du Roi — the King's kitchen garden at Versailles — was designed by Jean-Baptiste La Quintinie

The King and his courtiers were said to be particularly fond of the fresh peas grown there

VEGETABLE NAPKINS
pages 38–45

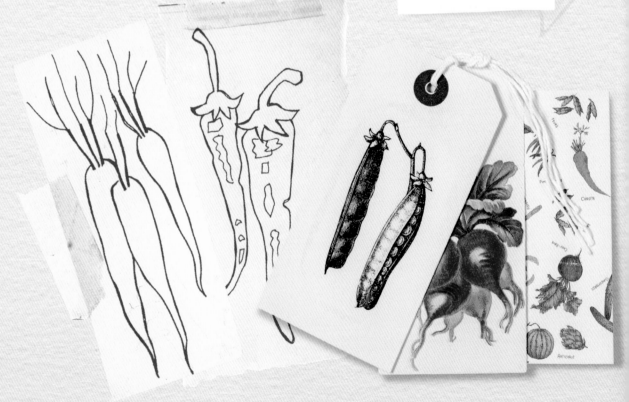

Finish off the
napkins with
a narrow
double hem
and a neat
miter at
each corner

Statue of
La Quintinie

Use raised satin stitch for smooth,
plump peas and feathery fly stitch
for the carrot foliage

Summer tote bag

.... with breezy seaside theme

Whether you're planning a vacation on the beach or simply dreaming of the summer, this seaside tote bag will brighten up any day. The cheerful nautical motifs are spread informally across a background of upholstery-weight cotton. This is an unconventional choice for embroidery, but the neutral colors are a perfect foil for the bright primary threads. Check your local furnishing-fabric store for similar striped fabrics. The square weave makes it easy to work regular parallel rows of satin stitch for the stripes. The bag is lined with a contrasting plain cotton to give it extra strength.

Finished size
About 12½ x 14½ inches (32 x 37 cm), plus 8¾ inches (22 cm) for the handles

You will need

* **Templates** on pages 164–165
* **48 x 21½ inches (120 x 55 cm) striped furnishing-weight fabric** for outer bag
* **27½ x 16 inches (70 x 40 cm) plain cotton fabric** for lining
* **Stranded embroidery thread** in five colors: red, golden yellow, charcoal, royal blue, and white (we used Sajou Retors du Nord in 2030 red; 2529 gold; 2086 coal; 2003 pure white; and 2879 agate)
* **Colored thread** for basting
* **Sewing thread** to match fabric
* **Basic sewing kit** (see pages 14–16)

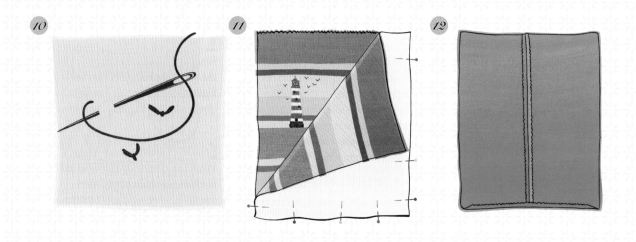

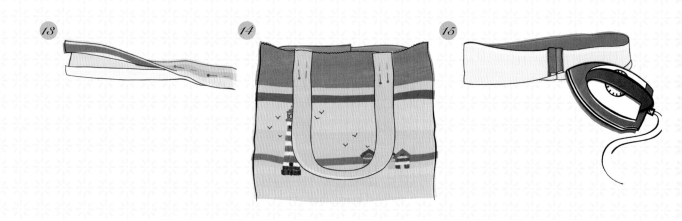

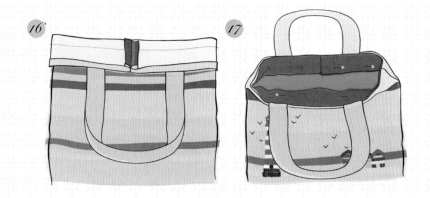

10

Pull the various elements of the design together by adding a scattered flock of seagulls. These are single fly stitches worked in charcoal thread; vary the size and angle of each one for a naturalistic look. The tiny shell is outlined in charcoal chain stitch and filled with golden yellow chain stitch.

Press the finished embroidery lightly from the wrong side, cushioning the stitches on a folded towel or padded ironing board cover.

Making up the bag

11

With right sides together, pin and baste the front and back of the bag together along the side and bottom edges. Machine stitch, using a ⅝-inch (1.5-cm) seam allowance. Clip the corners (see page 22) and press the seam allowances so that they lie over the bag. Turn the bag right side out.

12

Mark the center top edge of the lining with a small notch, then fold the fabric in half widthwise, at the notch. Pin and baste the side edges together, then machine stitch, using a ⅜-inch (1-cm) seam allowance. Press the seam open, then fold the resulting tube in half so that the seam line matches up with the notch. Stitch along the bottom edge, using a ⅜-inch (1-cm) seam allowance. Clip the corners and press the seam allowance inward, over the lining.

With wrong sides together, slip the lining inside the bag so that the seam line lies at the back of the bag. Push the corners down. Baste the outer bag and lining together around the top edge.

13

Press under a ⅜-inch (1-cm) turning along each long edge of the two handle strips. Fold the strips in half lengthwise, so that the folded edges match exactly, and press again. Pin and baste the two edges together, then machine stitch ⅛ inch (3 mm) from each long edge.

14

Pin and then baste the ends of the handles to the front and back of the bag, positioning the outside edges of the handles 3½ inches (9 cm) from the corners.

15

With right sides facing together, pin and baste the short ends of the long facing strip together, then machine stitch, using a ⅝-inch (1.5-cm) seam allowance. Press the seam open, then press under a ⅝-inch (1.5-cm) turning around one long edge of the resulting loop.

16

Slip the facing over the bag so that the seam lines up with the seam in the lining and the raw edges match up. Baste all three layers together. Machine stitch twice around the opening, using a ¾-inch (2-cm) seam allowance.

17

Turn the facing over to the inside of the bag so that it covers all the raw edges. Ease the seam line down so that it lies ⅙ to ⅛ inch (2 to 3 mm) below the top edge. Baste the neatened edge to the bag and machine stitch ⅛ inch (3 mm) from the fold. Stitch around the opening ⅛ inch (3 mm) from the top edge to finish off.

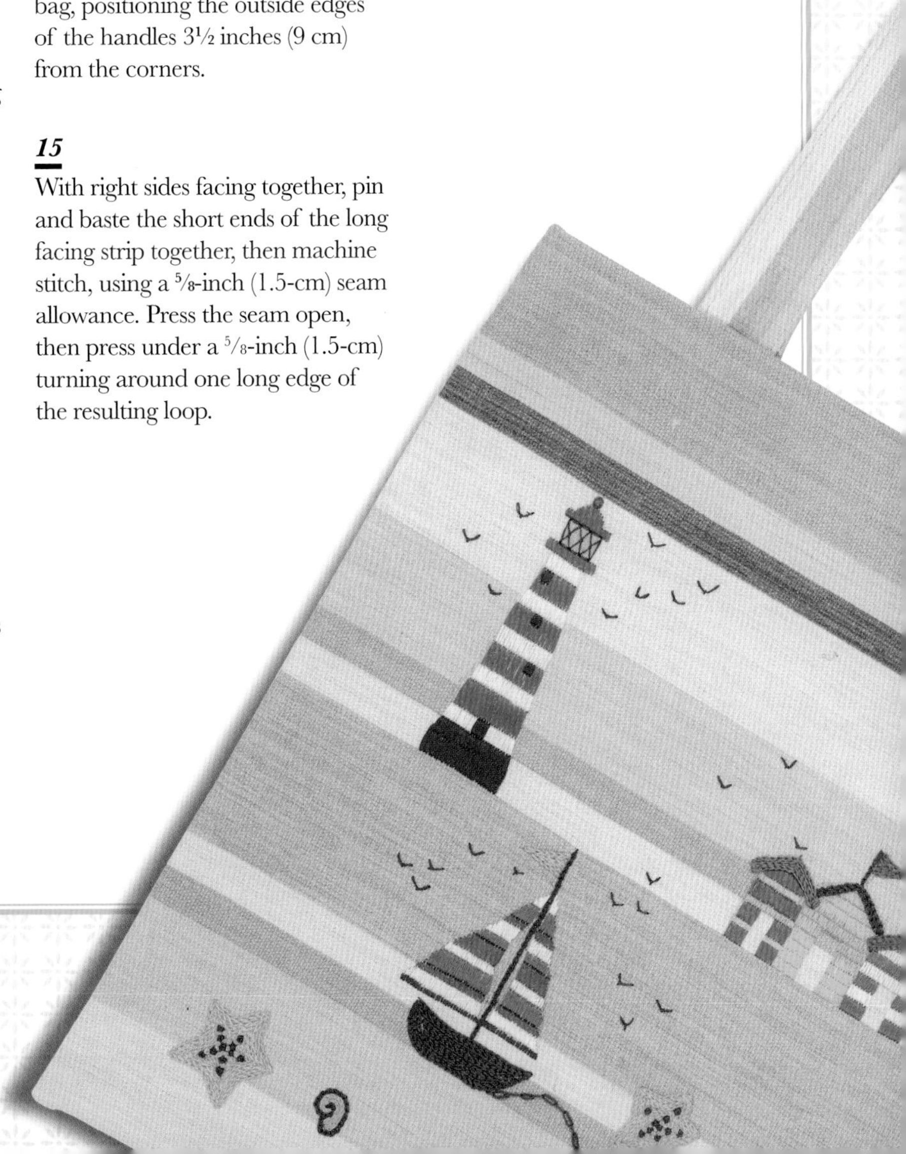

Twenties clutch bag

.... with a geometric cross-stitch design

All cross-stitch is based on a square grid, which makes it particularly suitable for geometric patterns, such as the appliquéd motif on this simple evening clutch. This symmetrical design draws its inspiration from the glamorous Jazz Age jewelry of the 1920s, with its brightly cut emeralds, pavé set diamonds, and angular shapes. Metallic threads and soft velvet complete the authentically vintage look. The bag itself is straightforward to put together and the proportions can easily be adapted if you want to make a bag in a different size or shape.

Finished size
....
9 x 6 inches (23 x 15 cm)

You will need
....
* *14 x 17¾ inches (35 x 45 cm) velvet*
* *14 x 13½ inches (35 x 34 cm) heavyweight fusible interfacing*
* *14 x 17¾ inches (35 x 45 cm) dress-weight cotton fabric* for lining
* *5½-inch (14-cm) square of white 32-count linen*
* *Chart* on page 175
* *Stranded metallic embroidery thread* in two colors: emerald blue and palest blue (we used Sajou Tonkin in 1017 emerald and 1011 sky blue)
* *Stranded embroidery thread* in dark blue (we used Sajou Retors du Nord, 2964 navy)
* *⅝-inch (15-mm) sew-on magnetic bag clasp*
* *Colored thread* for basting
* *Sewing thread* to match fabric
* *Basic sewing kit* (see pages 14–16)

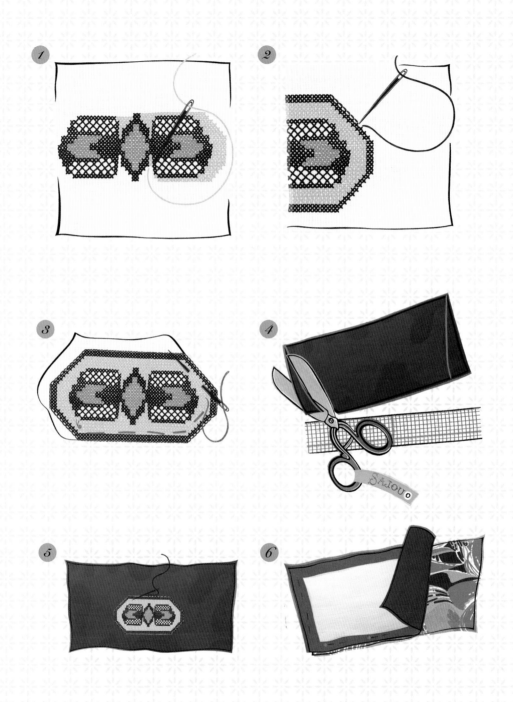

The Projects

Cutting out the fabric

FROM VELVET, CUT:

* **Flap: one 10 x 5-inch (25 x 12-cm) rectangle**
* **Main bag: one 10 x 12-inch (25 x 30-cm) rectangle**

FROM LINING FABRIC, CUT:

* **Flap lining: one 10 x 5-inch (25 x 12-cm) rectangle**
* **Inner lining: two 10 x 6½-inch (25 x 16-cm) rectangles**

Embroidering the motif

1
Fold the linen into quarters to find the center point. Following the chart on page 175 and using cross-stitch (see page 26), work the center diamond in emerald blue, then stitch the entire decorative frame with three strands of dark blue. Add the other two "emeralds." Fill in the background with pale blue.

2
Work the outside edge in three strands of dark blue. Finish off with a line of dark blue backstitch (see page 29) along the straight edges and half-cross stitches (see page 26) along the diagonal corners.

3
Trim the linen so that there is a ⅜-inch (1-cm) margin all around the motif. Fold this surplus fabric to the wrong side and baste it in place.

TIP

If you are using Sajou Tonkin thread, use a single strand throughout; if you are using a different metallic thread, use two strands throughout.

Making up the bag

4
Place the velvet flap right side down. Mark a point on each side edge of the flap ¾ inch (2 cm) down from the top corners. Mark a point on the lower edge, ¾ inch (2 cm) in from each bottom corner on either side. Using a ruler and an air-erasable marking pen, draw a line between these points on each side of the flap and cut along them.

5
Pin the motif centered on the flap, ¾ inch (2 cm) up from the lower edge. Slip-stitch in place, using a single strand of the dark blue embroidery thread.

Cut two pieces of interfacing, one ⅝ inch (1.5 cm) smaller all around than the flap and one ⅝ inch (1.5 cm) smaller all around than the bag. Press them to the wrong side of their respective pieces of velvet, following the manufacturer's instructions.

6
Trim the lining flap to the same size as the flap. With right sides facing, pin and baste the two together along the side and bottom edges. Set your machine to a ⅛-inch (3-mm) straight stitch and thread with matching sewing thread. Using a ⅝-inch (1-cm) seam allowance, machine stitch along the basted edges.

Clip the corners (see page 22) and turn the flap right side out. Ease out the corners, press lightly from the wrong side, and baste the two top edges together.

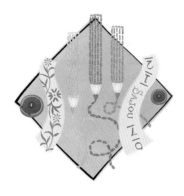

Portable pencil holder

.... _with simple stitchery_

Get your kids ready for a new school year or the long summer vacation with this useful pencil holder. It's a great project if you are learning how to stitch or have just acquired a sewing machine. Only the most basic embroidery stitches—running stitch, backstitch, and straight stitch—are used and all the machined seams are perfectly straight. You can copy our curly "pencil lines" exactly as they appear on the template, or have fun drawing your own wiggles. Try personalizing the holder by adding an embroidered name, or make one of the pencil lines into a flower, simple car, or airplane shape.

Finished size
....

10 inches (25 cm) square

You will need
....

* _**Templates**_ on page 168–169
* _**Two 10-inch (25-cm) squares of mid-weight blue fabric**_
* _**Stranded embroidery thread**_ in four colors: bright yellow, red, turquoise green, and light brown (we used Sajou Retors du Nord in 2021 celadon; 2033 gladiola; 2043 sulfur; and 2780 ecru)
* _**5 x 10-inches (12 x 25-cm) striped fabric**_; we used Sajou Cannes fabric in color scheme 2
* _**5 feet (150 cm) dark blue bias binding**_
* _**Sewing thread**_ to match fabric
* _**Colored thread**_ for basting
* _**10-inch (25-cm) square of fusible interfacing**_
* _**32 inches (80 cm) narrow ribbon**_; we used Sajou Meter ribbon in red
* _**Blue button**_, ¾ inch (2 cm) in diameter
* _**Basic sewing kit**_ (see pages 14–16)

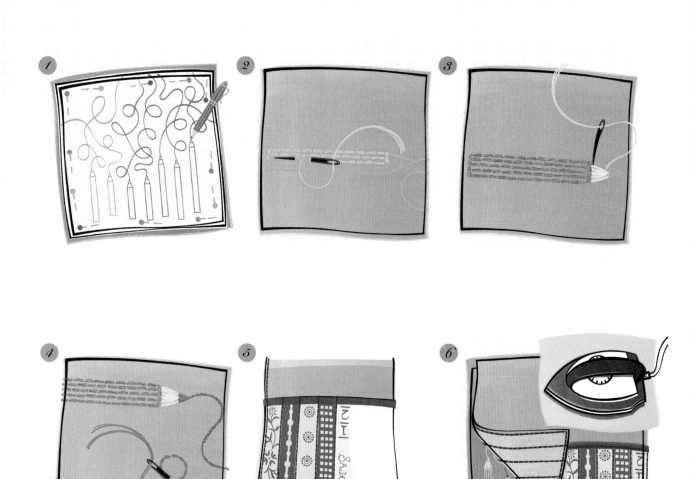

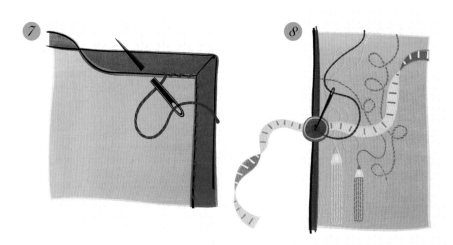

Embroidering the motifs

Trace the first part of the full-size templates from pages 168–169 onto the bottom right corner of the tracing paper. Line up the two small crosses on the second part of the template with the second pencil and trace off the second outline to complete the image.

1

Place a piece of white dressmaker's carbon paper on one of the squares of blue fabric, carbon side down. Position the tracing paper centered on top, then pin the layers together. Carefully draw over all of the pencil lines with a ball-point pen.

2

Embroider the motifs as instructed below, using four strands of thread throughout; you can find details of how to work all the stitches on pages 28–35. Work backstitch along each of the five lines marked along each pencil and also along the short ends. From left to right, use the following colors: bright yellow, red, turquoise green, bright yellow, red, turquoise green, yellow.

3

Fill in the wooden part of each pencil point with several slanting straight stitches, using a light brown thread.

4

Embroider the tips of the pencils in straight stitch, and then along the wiggly pencil lines in thread colors to match the pencil barrels. Use running stitch for the three bright yellow pencils, whipped backstitch for the red pencils, and backstitch for the turquoise-green lines.

Making the pocket

Neaten the top edge of the striped fabric with bias binding, sewing it on either by hand or machine (see page 21).

5

With both fabrics right side up, pin and then baste the striped fabric to the second blue square, aligning the side and bottom edges. Using a ¼-inch (5-mm) seam, machine stitch the two pieces together around the side and bottom edges. Divide the striped fabric into sections by machine stitching along the edges of the stripes, sewing from the lower edge toward the binding and reinforcing the end of each line of stitches with a few reverse stitches. (If you are using a different fabric, these lines need to be ⅝ inch / 1.5 cm apart.)

Assembling the pencil roll

6

Following the manufacturer's instructions, press the fusible interfacing on to the wrong side of the pocket square. Peel off the backing paper. Place the outer square, right side down, on your ironing board and lay the pocket square, right side up, on top, carefully matching the corners. Press in place.

7

Trim the fabric if it is not perfectly squared off. Starting and finishing at the center top edge, bind all the way around the outside with bias binding, neatly mitering the corners (see page 21). As with the pocket, you can sew the binding on by hand or machine.

8

Fold the ribbon in half, then stitch this midpoint to the binding on the outside of the pencil roll, at the center of the left side edge. Sew the button securely over the seam.

Provençal tablecloth

.... *with lavender garland*

Lavender has been called "the soul of Provence." Nothing epitomizes high summer in the South of France more than the vast swathes of this fragrant plant that fill the fields at harvest time, and the vivid color has long inspired artists and writers alike. The entwined lavender stems at the center of this fine linen cloth are made up of four identical quarter sections that join together to make a continuous garland. The curved stems are embroidered in stem stitch and the naturalistic flowers are worked with lazy daisy stitch, in two shades of lavender thread.

You will need

* **White linen tablecloth**, about 40 inches (100 cm) square
* **Stranded embroidery thread** in three colors: lavender, mauve, and jade green (we used Sajou Retors du Nord 2008 lupin; 2302 mauve; and 2717 jade)
* **Template** on page 167
* **Basic sewing kit** (see pages 14–16)

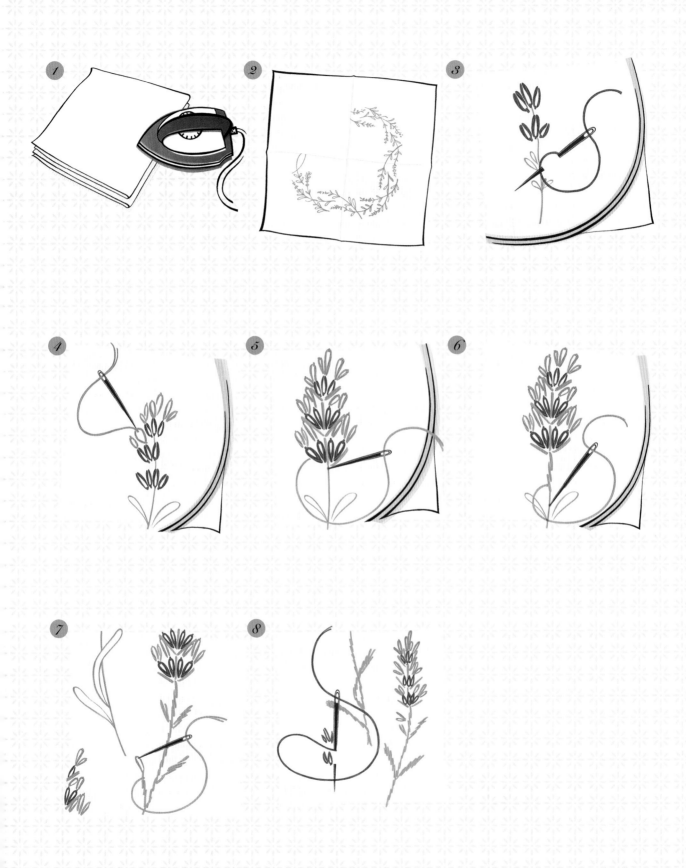

Transferring the outline

1

If you are using a new tablecloth, wash and iron it first to allow for any shrinkage and to remove the fabric sizing. Fold it into quarters and lightly press the creases to mark the four quarters.

2

Trace the full-size template on page 167. Following the instructions on page 24, transfer the outline onto the fabric four times, once in each quarter. The stems and flower heads will meet up across the seams to complete the design.

Embroidering the flower heads

3

Embroider the motifs as instructed below; you can find details of how to work all of the stitches on pages 28–35. For the buds, thread the needle with three strands of lavender thread and work a detached chain stitch for each bud, working from top to bottom.

4

For the petals, thread the needle with two strands of mauve thread and work one, two, or three detached chain stitches at the tip of each bud, sewing in the opposite direction, from bottom to top.

5

For the sepals, thread the needle with two strands of jade green thread. Work a slanting straight stitch on each side of the top group of buds, then work a straight stitch down to the next group. Repeat this two or three times until you reach the bottom of the flower head.

Embroidering the stem & leaves

6

Using two strands of jade thread work along the curved stem in stem stitch, just as far as the first pair of leaves, carefully following the outline to create a smooth curve.

7

Fill in the leaf outlines with several closely spaced straight stitches, angling them to follow the direction of the leaves. Complete the rest of the stem and the other leaves in the same way.

8

Work the remaining stems in the same way to complete the garland. Press the finished embroidery lightly from the wrong side with a dry iron, cushioning it on a folded dish towel or padded ironing board cover so that the stitches do not become flattened.

Dandelion crib sheet

.... *with lace trim*

Young children have always learned to tell the time by blowing repeatedly on a dandelion clock until every single seed has disappeared. Hopefully, it will always be time to go to sleep when baby is tucked under this lace-trimmed crib sheet.

The delicate seeds are scattered randomly across the border in a naturalistic drift; you can mark the positions first with an air-erasable pen, if you prefer. The template gives the outline for the two dandelion heads and the positions of the seeds that lie closest to them. You can extend the design out to the right and left so that it is the correct width for your sheet, spacing the seeds more widely apart toward the outside and top edges and varying their direction.

Finished size

30 x 40 inches (75 x 100 cm)

You will need

* *8-inch (20-cm) strip of white cotton sheeting* for the edging strip, 2 inches (5 cm) wider than the sheet
* *Templates* on page 165
* *Stranded embroidery thread* in five colors: light green, light brown, blue-green, silvery mid-gray, and pale gray (we used Sajou Retors du Nord in 2443 alicante; 2780 ecru; 2449 nile; 2001 cloud; and 2180 metal)
* *Sewing thread* to match fabric
* *Colored thread* for basting
* *32 inches (80 cm) lace edging*; we used Sajou guipure no. 1
* *Store-bought crib sheet*, about 30 x 40 inches (75 x 100 cm)
* *Optional name tape or woven label*; we used "Enfants" from the Sajou household ribbon collection
* *Basic sewing kit* (see pages 14–16)

The dandelion traditionally
symbolizes happiness, abundance,
and new beginnings

Scatter
the embroidered
seeds for a natural, wind-blown feel

TARAXACUM OFFICINALI

Use just a single strand
of embroidery thread for
a delicate look

Stitches
* Raised satin stitch gives
  depth to the stems
* French knots for texture
* Angled satin stitch for
  a smooth stem

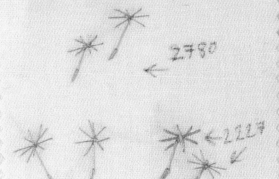

2780

←2227

2780

Embroidery thread colors

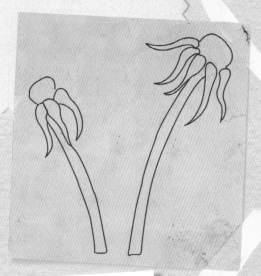

DANDELION
CRIB SHEET
pages 66 – 71

Butterfly collection

.... *with three classic motifs*

Butterflies of all shapes and sizes have long been favorite subjects for textile artists. There is something inherently pleasing about the natural symmetry of their wings and the beautiful patterns give great scope for interpretation in embroidery stitches and fine threads. This handsome blue specimen is mounted in a picture frame in ecologically sound imitation of museum cases, but it would look equally effective as a single motif on a bag, scarf, cushion, or crib cover. Inspiration for the design came from Sajou's collection of butterfly-print thread winders; why not search other illustrations and design your own interpretation of a classic?

Finished size
....
8 inches (20 cm)

You will need
....
* *Templates* on page 166
* *8-inch (20-cm) square of off-white linen*
* *Basic sewing kit* (see pages 14–16)

FOR THE BLUE BUTTERFLY:

* *Stranded embroidery threads* in four shades of blue: azure, gray-blue, sapphire blue, and turquoise (we used Sajou Retors du Nord in 2010 azure; 2818 gobelin blue; 2882 sapphire; and 2011 turquoise)

Stranded embroidery threads for the two smaller butterflies are listed on pages 75 and 77.

Sajou threa[d]

Butterflies have
long been a favorite
subject for designers

Monogrammed sachets

.... *with cross-stitch alphabet*

The cross-stitch alphabet that inspired these three scented sachets first appeared in *Dessins de Broderies, Album 171.* This was just one of the many beautifully engraved pattern books that Sajou published during the nineteenth century, when large-scale decorative letters were used to monogram household linen. In every French household, the owner's initials would be skillfully embroidered onto towels, pillowcases, and sheets.

The combination of swirling copperplate capitals and floral embellishments gives this particular alphabet a timeless appeal. It can be stitched in a single thread, as originally printed, or you could add more detail to the design by picking out the flowers and leaves in colors to match the border fabric.

Finished size
....

5 inches (12.5 cm) square

You will need
....

FOR EACH SACHET

* *16 x 6½ inches (40 x 16 cm) flower print cotton fabric*

* *5½-inch (14-cm) square 32-count linen* (see right for color)

* *Charts* on pages 172–174

* *1 card of Sajou Retors du Nord stranded embroidery thread* (see right for color)

* *Sewing thread* to match fabric

* *Colored thread* for basting

* *Fine cross-stitch needle*

* *12 x 6½ inches (30 x 16 cm) plain white cotton fabric*

* *Handful of dried flowers* or potpourri

* *Basic sewing kit* (see pages 14–16)

FOR SACHET 1

* *Thread*: 2007 blackcurrant

* *Linen*: lime tree

FOR SACHET 2

* *Thread*: 2000 undyed

* *Linen*: thyme

FOR SACHET 3

* *Thread*: 2086 coal

* *Linen*: sepia

Daisy-dot gadget case

.... *with quilted effect*

This softly padded cover is designed to hold a tablet computer, but the basic pattern can easily be scaled up or down to make a case that will fit a cell phone, a large laptop, or even a pencil case.

The polka dot linen, with its pattern of large white dots, makes the perfect background for the embroidered daisies. You can vary their size and color, and scatter them randomly, as here, or space them more regularly for a more ordered look. The case is lined with matching fabric and the zipper fastening means that it fits snugly to protect your gadget when you're on the move.

You will need

* ***Two rectangles of polka-dot print fabric***, 2 inches (5 cm) larger all around than your gadget; we used Sajou white polka-dot linen

* ***Stranded embroidery thread*** in four colors: fuchsia pink, bright yellow, orange, and ivory (we used Sajou Retors du Nord in 2026 fuchsia; 2043 sulfur; 2405 orange; and 2196 ivory)

* ***Two rectangles of contrasting cotton fabric*** for the lining, 2 inches (5 cm) larger all around than your gadget

* ***Two rectangles of cotton batting***, 2 inches (5 cm) larger all around than your gadget

* ***Contrasting nylon zipper***, about 2½ inches (6 cm) longer than your gadget

* ***5 feet (1.5 m) bias binding***

* ***Sewing thread*** to match linen and zipper

* ***Colored thread*** for basting

* ***Sheet of dressmaker's pattern paper***

* ***Quilter's safety pins***

* ***Basic sewing kit*** (see pages 14–16)

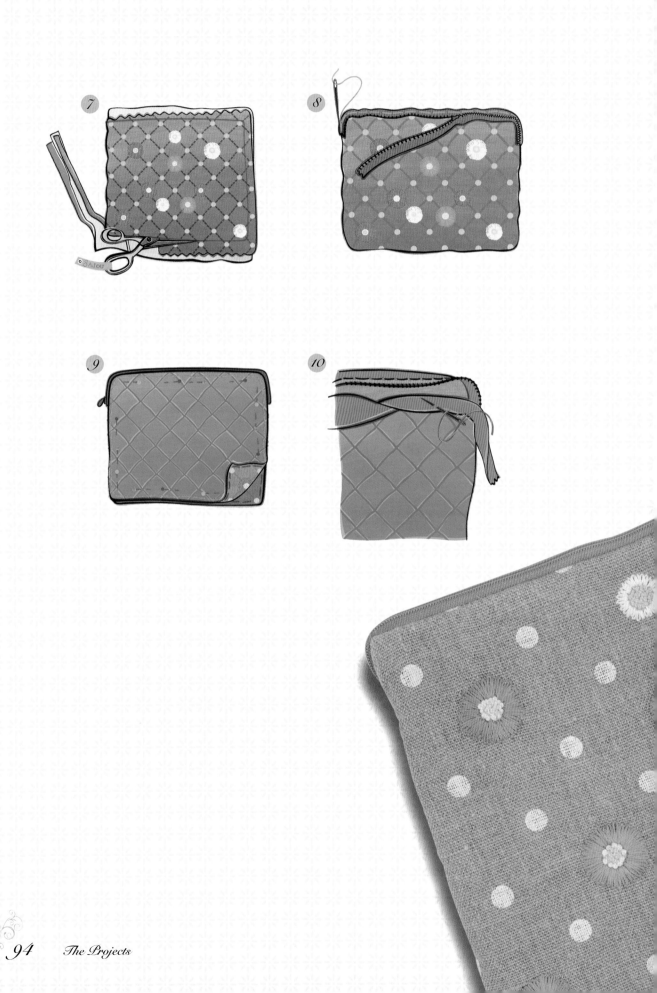

Assembling
the gadget case

7

Remove the pins, then baste around the outside edge, ¼ inch (5 mm) in from the outline. Cut out around the outline. Make the back of the case in exactly the same way, omitting the embroidery.

8

Matching the center points and with right sides facing, pin and then baste one side of the zipper to the bag front. Make sure that the open end lies at the left and match the edge of the zipper tape to the edge of the quilted fabric. Sew the zipper in place (see page 23).

9

Keeping the zipper open, pin and baste the side and bottom edges of the front and back together. Make sure that the ends of the zipper tapes are on the outside, then machine stitch ⅜ inch (1 cm) from the edge. Reinforce both ends of the seam with a few extra stitches.

10

Trim the seam allowance back to ¼ inch (5 mm). Bind (see page 21) the two top edges and then the side and bottom edges with bias binding to conceal all the raw edges. Sew it on by hand, with small secure slip stitches. Turn the bag right side out and press lightly, placing a clean cloth over the top to protect the embroidery.

Silk slipper bag

.... *with dainty cross-stitch motif*

The magnificent Palace of Versailles lies at the end of a wide, tree-lined avenue in a historic suburb to the south of Paris. Just a short walk from the palace, hidden away within a historic courtyard, is the Maison Sajou showroom. This treasure trove of sewing notions is filled with the most amazing array of threads, linen, pattern books, needle cases, embroidery scissors, tape measures, and other needlework tools … So when it came to designing a cross-stitch motif for this drawstring shoe bag, there could only be one source of inspiration: a pair of silk slippers belonging to Marie Antoinette, queen of France and former resident of Versailles!

Finished size
....
9 x 15 inches (23 x 38 cm)

You will need
....
* *40 x 20 inches (100 x 50 cm) printed cotton fabric* for the bag
* *40 x 20 inches (100 x 50 cm) plain cotton fabric* for the lining
* *Chart* on page 175
* *Stranded embroidery threads* in four shades: green-yellow, dusky pink, shell pink, and medium turquoise (we used Maison Sajou Retors du Nord in 2034 moss; 2469 rosewood; 2535 blush; and 2777 emerald)
* *8 x 6 inches (20 x 15 cm) off-white 32-count embroidery linen*
* *Colored thread* for basting
* *Sewing thread* to match fabric
* *60 inches (150 cm) ribbon*, ¾ inch (2 cm) wide, for the ties
* *Basic sewing kit* (see pages 14–16)

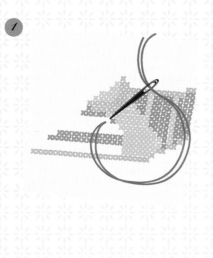

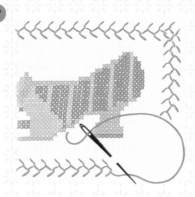

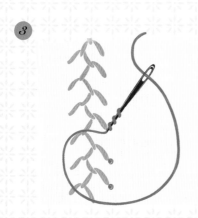

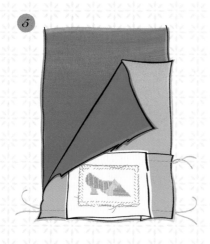

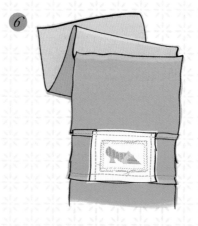

Cutting out

FROM PRINTED COTTON
FABRIC, CUT:

* **One 10 x 8-inch (25 x 20-cm)
  rectangle** for the top front
* **Two 2¾ x 4¼-inch
  (7 x 11-cm) border strips**
* **One 10 x 17½-inch
  (25 x 45-cm) rectangle**
  for the main bag

FROM PLAIN COTTON
FABRIC, CUT:

* **Two 10 x 17½-inch
  (25 x 45-cm) rectangles**
  for the lining

Stitching the shoe

1

Fold the linen into quarters to find the center point (see page 26). Following the chart on page 175, embroider the shoe onto the linen rectangle, using the colors indicated. Position the motif in the center and embroider it as instructed below, using two strands of thread throughout; you can find details of how to work the stitches on pages 28–35.

2

Frame the shoe with four rows of dusky pink feather stitch (see page 31), worked a generous ¼ inch (8 mm) away from the shoe. To keep the stitches regular, count six threads across and three threads down for each "v" shape.

3

Complete the border by working a turquoise French knot (see page 34) at the end of each outside "branch" of the feather stitches. To make these extra round and beadlike, wrap the thread three times around the shaft of the needle and insert the point in the same hole from which it emerged. Pull through gently so that the knot sits on the surface.

Press the finished embroidery lightly from the wrong side, cushioning it on a folded towel or padded ironing board cover. Trim it down to 6 x 4¼ inches (15 x 11 cm), so that there is a ¾-inch (2-cm) margin along each edge.

Making up the bag

4

Use ⅜-inch (1-cm) seam allowances throughout. To make the center panel, with right sides together, pin a border strip to each side edge of the embroidered linen. Baste in place, then machine stitch. Press the seam allowances toward the border strips.

5

Again with the right sides together, pin the top front to the top edge of the center panel and the main bag to the bottom edge. Baste and then machine stitch the two seams. Press both seams away from the center panel.

6

With right sides together, pin and baste the two lining rectangles to the top and bottom edges of the bag to make a long strip. Machine stitch, then press the seams toward the lining fabric.

Measure and draw on a point on each side edge of the lining, ¾ inch (2 cm) above the seam, on the wrong side of the fabric. These points mark the openings for the gathering channel.

Now fold the whole strip in half lengthwise, with the right sides facing inward. Match up the points where the seams meet at the top of the bag and pin them together. Pin the corners, then add more pins all the way along the side and top edges. Baste the edges together.

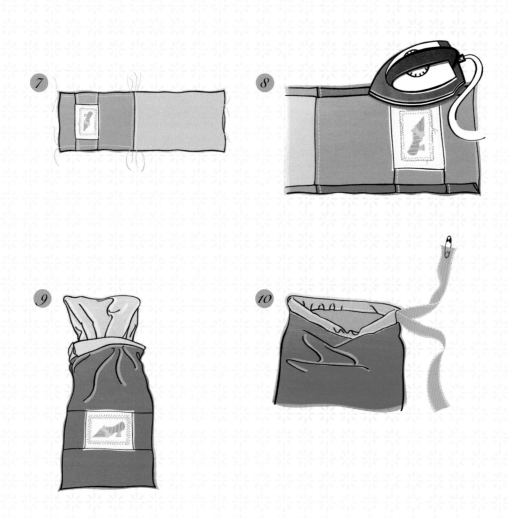

7

Machine stitch around the three pinned edges. You need to leave three gaps in the seam: a ¾-inch (2-cm) one on each side edge, between the seam and your pencil mark, and a 6-inch (15-cm) space at the short edge of the lining, for turning through.

8

Trim each corner to within ⅛ inch (3 mm) of the seam line (see page 22) and then press all the seam allowances (including those along the gaps) inward.

9

Turn the whole bag right side out through the 6-inch (15-cm) gap. Ease out the seams and corners of the main bag. Pin the two neatened edges of the gap together and machine across them. Push the lining right inside the bag, making sure that it fits neatly into the bottom corners.

Adjust the opening so that ¾ inch (2 cm) of the lining projects beyond the seam line. This will be the gathering channel. Baste it in place, then machine stitch close to the seam.

10

Cut the ribbon in half. Fasten a safety pin to the end of one length and feed it through one of the side gaps. Push it all around the gathering channel and back out of the gap. Thread the second ribbon through the other hole in the same way. Knot both ends of each ribbon together, leaving 2-inch (5-cm) tails, and trim each tail into a "v" shape.

Portrait from the Musée Carnavalet

Soft sugar almond shades reflect the subtle silk shades worn by the court at Versailles

Don't forget to add a gleaming pearl button

SILK SLIPPER BAG

pages 96–103

The Louis heel, with its elegant curve, was worn by both men and women

Marie Antoinette's shoes were trimmed with buckles, bows, pleated ribbon, and lace

old cut steel shoe buckle

sumptuous lace ruffle

This antique shoe-
shaped snuff box
dates from the early
nineteenth century

Create a dense
brocade-like effect
by working the stripes
in cross-stitch

Garlanded lampshade

.... with tonal embroidery

Despite the wide range of lighting available in design stores and online, finding the perfect lampshade can sometimes seem like an impossible task. Re-covering an existing shade with new fabric to match your design scheme is, however, a surprisingly straightforward project. Adding a hand-embroidered border in a darker shade of the same color will make it truly unique. The rambling rose design on this sophisticated shade is made up of a single repeated motif that can be easily adapted to fit a cylindrical or conical lampshade in any size.

You will need

* **Plain cardboard or fabric-covered cardboard lampshade** with wire frame
* **Template** on page 177
* **Rectangle of 32-count linen** in slate gray, 4 inches (10 cm) wider and deeper than paper pattern
* **Stranded embroidery thread** in dark charcoal (we used Sajou Retors du Nord in 2086 coal)
* **Reel of ½-inch- (12-mm-) wide double-sided tape**
* **Glue stick**
* **Basic sewing kit** (see pages 14–16)

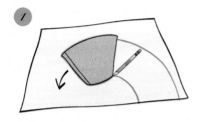

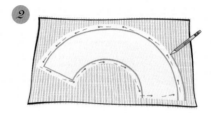

Preparing the linen

1

Position your shade on the paper so that the vertical seam is lined up against the bottom right edge. Carefully roll the shade over to the left, marking the path of the top and bottom rims onto the paper, until the seam meets the paper again. Join the top and bottom lines at this point.

2

Add another 1¼ inches (3 cm) to the top and bottom edges, and an extra ⅝ inch (1.5 cm) at the second straight edges, then cut out along the pencil lines. Wrap the pattern around the shade to check that it fits properly and then adjust the curves, if necessary.

Pin the paper pattern to the linen and draw carefully around the outside edge using a chalk pencil. Remove the pattern.

3

Trace the template from page 178 onto thick tracing paper and pin to the bottom left edge of the shade outline, 1½ inches (4 cm) up from the curved line. Slip a small piece of dressmaker's carbon paper underneath and draw over the template with a ball-point pen.

4

Repin the template to the right of the first motif, still 1½ inches (4 cm) up from the curve, so that the stem appears to grow from the center of the rose. Draw over the outline once again, then continue in the same way around the entire bottom edge. Fill in the space at the left with an extra rose and add more leaves to fill up any gaps at the right.

Working the embroidery

5

Mount the first section of the design in an embroidery hoop (the size of the hoop will depend on the size of your lampshade.) Using two strands of charcoal thread, embroider over the stems in small backstitches (see page 29). Fill in the leaves and the dots with satin stitch (see page 32), angling each stitch to fit within the outline.

6

The five rose petals are worked in satin stitch, and the stitches within each one are angled from the center top of the petal toward the middle of the flower. Work three small straight stitches (see page 33) in the center space.

TIP

• *If your shade is much lighter than the new fabric, you may need to cover it with an extra layer of fabric to prevent the original color from showing through the linen.*

• *Make your paper pattern before buying the fabric, so you will know exactly how much you need.*

SAFETY FIRST

Before you work, spray the linen with a fire retardant and let dry completely. Only use a low-energy lightbulb, which emits low levels of heat, with the shade.

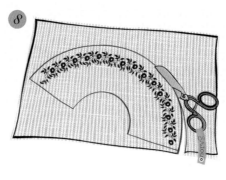

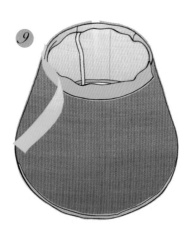

Making up
the shade

7

Continue embroidering each motif in the same way. Keep the back of the work as neat as you can, because any stray threads will show through when the shade is illuminated.

8

Press the finished embroidery lightly from the wrong side. Cut out the lampshade cover using a pair of long scissors, carefully following the outline.

9

Bind the top and bottom rims of the shade with double-side tape, using short lengths to fit comfortably around the curves. Peel off the backing paper. Stick a length of tape to the back of the left and right edges.

10

Wrap the cover around the shade, lining the left edge up with the vertical seam and making sure that there is an equal margin projecting at top and bottom. Overlap the right edge and smooth down. Snip into the top margin at the point where each strut meets the top edge and fold the fabric over the tape. You may need to secure the edges with a glue stick.

11

Neaten the bottom edge in the same way, gluing down any loose fabric with a little dab of the adhesive.

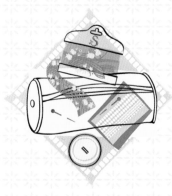

Bordered bolster

.... *with pulled and drawn threadwork*

This sophisticated piped linen bolster is decorated with bands of drawn and pulled threadwork, two closely related techniques that are classified as "openwork." "Drawn threadwork" involves pulling out strands of the background fabric to create a lacy look, while "pulled thread" stitches tightly bunch up the woven threads to create a regular pattern of small holes. Traditionally stitched in white thread on fine white material, they were used to embellish pillowcases, sheet headings, baby wear, and tablecloths. As with the tray cloth on page 138, we have updated the look by using colored threads to match the linen and lily-of-the-valley ribbon.

Finished size
....
16 x 6 inches (40 x 15 cm)

You will need
....

* *40 x 27½ inches (100 x 70 cm) 32-count linen* in pale blue; we used Sajou embroidery linen in azure
* *40 x 27½ inches (100 x 70 cm) white cotton dress-weight fabric*
* *6 x 3¼ inches (16 x 8 cm) green velvet* or other green fabric to cover buttons
* *One 24-inch (60-cm) square of light green cotton fabric* to cover piping cord
* *Stranded embroidery threads* in three colors: pale blue, white and pale green (we used Sajou Retors du Nord in 2818 gobelin blue; 2003 grand blanc; and 2449 nil)
* *40 inches (1 m) ribbon, 4 cm (1½ inches) wide;* we used Sajou Muguet Ciel
* *Colored thread* for basting
* *Sewing thread* to match fabric
* *48 inches (120 cm) piping cord,* ⅛ inch (4 mm) in diameter
* *Two self-cover buttons,* 1¼ inches (3 cm) in diameter
* *16 x 6-inch (40 x 15-cm) bolster cushion pad*
* *Basic sewing kit* (see pages 14–16)

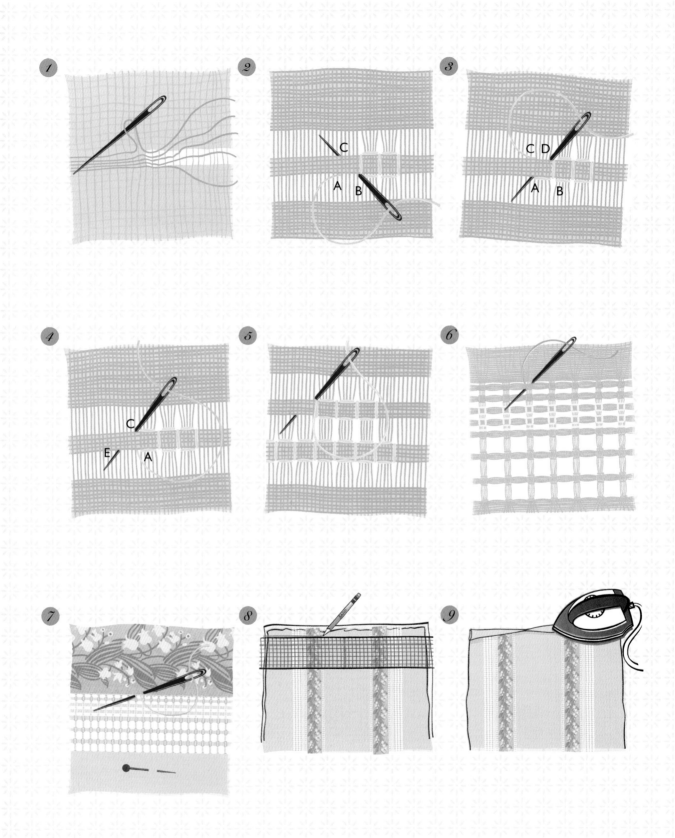

Cutting out

FROM BLUE LINEN AND WHITE COTTON, CUT:

* **One 17 x 19-inch (43 x 48-cm) rectangle**
* **Two circles 6¾ inches (17 cm) in diameter**

FROM BLUE LINEN, CUT:

* **Two 16½ x 2½-inch (42 x 6-cm) strips**

FROM GREEN VELVET OR OTHER FABRIC, CUT:

* **Two 2½-inch (6-cm) circles** to cover the buttons

FROM LIGHT GREEN COTTON FABRIC, CUT:

* **Bias strips 1½ inches (4 cm) wide** to cover piping cord (see page 22)

Stitching the openwork

1
Mark a point on the bottom (17-inch/43-cm) edge of the blue linen rectangle, 3¼ inches (8 cm) in from the left corner. Carefully remove the five vertical threads that lie inward from the point. Using a large tapestry needle, lift the ends out of the fabric and then gently ease them out at intervals along the width of the fabric. Work with the drawn threads along the left edge of the rectangle facing you.

2
Each of the seven rows of open work is worked in four-sided stitch, which is worked in three separate stages. To start the first row, thread a fine tapestry needle with two strands of pale blue thread and

fasten on ¾ inch (2 cm) in from the right edge. Bring the needle up at A, five threads down from the long horizontal space created by removing the threads. Count five threads to the right and take it down at B, then bring it back up between the open threads at C, directly above A.

3
Take the needle down five threads to the right to D, above B, and bring it out diagonally below at A.

4
Finally, reinsert the needle at C and bring it out diagonally at E, five threads to the left of A. Repeat the sequence of three stitches to the end of the row. Each time, you should pull up the thread slightly tighter than you would for a normal stitch. Mounting the fabric in an embroidery hoop will help to keep the tension regular, but it isn't essential.

5
Count five threads up from the completed first row of four-sided stitch, then pull out the next five horizontal threads, leaving a band of five threads in between the two spaces. Again using blue thread, work a second row of four-sided stitch along the five vertical threads between the gaps, following the same grouping as in the first line.

6
Work three more rows of four-sided stitch using two strands of white thread and one row using two strands of pale green thread.

These are worked in the same way as before, over blocks of five by five threads, but without removing any threads. Leave a gap of 1½ inches (4 cm) or the width of your ribbon, then work one more row of four-sided stitch in pale green thread.

Repeat steps 1–6, starting from the opposite edge of the fabric.

7
Press the finished embroidery lightly from the wrong side and pull into shape as necessary. Cut the ribbon in half and pin one length between each of the two rows of green stitches, with the pattern running from left to right. Slip-stitch it in place along each edge, using a single strand of pale blue thread. Press again from the wrong side.

Making up the cover

8
Tack the rectangle of white cotton fabric to the wrong side of the linen. The top and bottom edges of the linen will now look uneven. Tidy them up by ruling two horizontal lines across the fabric, ¾ inch (2 cm) in from each edge, and cutting through both layers. Rebaste, if necessary.

9
Press both narrow blue strips in half widthwise and pin them to the front top and bottom of the cover, matching the raw edges. Machine stitch ⅜ inch (1 cm) from the edge, then press the seam allowances so that they lie over the cover.

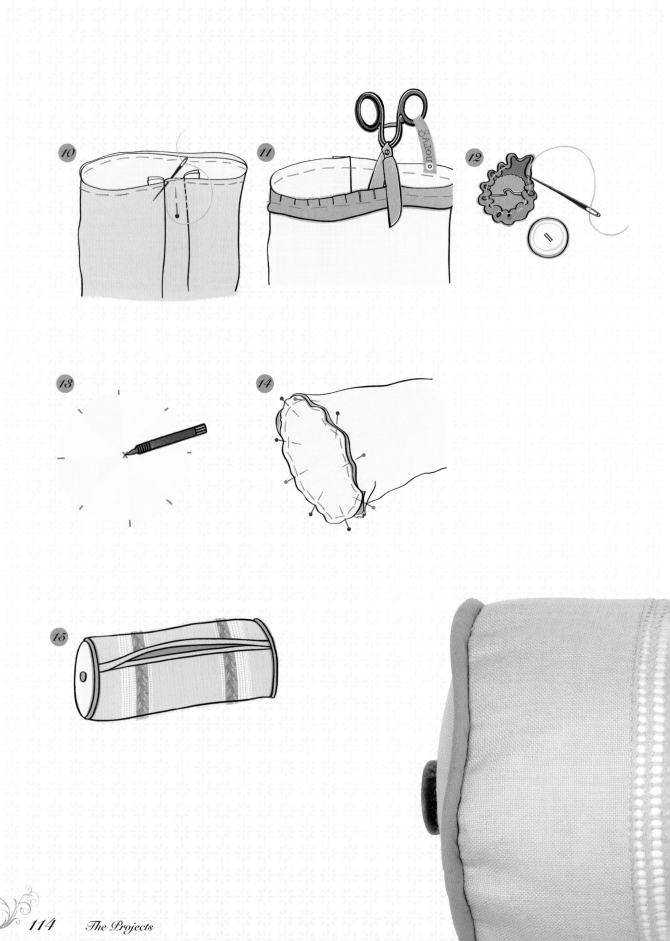

10

With the white cotton facing inward, fold the cover into a tube. Pin the two facings so that one overlaps the other. Slip-stitch the two together for ¾ inch (2 cm) along the folded edge at both ends of the cover and then along the outside edges.

11

Cut the piping cord in two and cover it with green cotton bias strips (see page 22). Tack one length of piping to each side opening in the cover tube, matching the joining in the piping up with the seam line (see pages 22–23). Make a series of vertical snips through the fabric and piping, cutting to within ¹/₁₆ inch (2 mm) of the cord.

12

To cover the buttons, stitch a round of small running stitches around the edge of each green circle. Gather up the thread, then slip the domed top of the self-cover button inside. Draw up completely and fasten off the thread. Slot the backplate of the cover into position so that the shank fits through the gap and press it firmly into position.

13

Pin, then baste the two blue linen circles to the circles of white cotton around the outside edges. Fold them four times to divide into eight equal sections and mark the ends of the folds. Mark the center, then press to remove any creases. Sew a button to the center of each circle.

14

Turn the cover inside out. Fold four times to create eight equal divisions, and mark the ends as for the circles. With right sides facing, pin a circle to each end of the cover tube, matching up the eight points around the circumference of the circles to the eight marks on the cover. Doing this helps ensure that the two fit together precisely.

15

With the blue circles facing inward, baste the circles in place at the ends of the cover tube, ³/₈ inch (1 cm) from the edge. Fit a zipper foot to your sewing machine and, with the cover uppermost, slowly and carefully machine stitch all the way around both ends, keeping the edge of the foot close to the piping cord. Turn the cover right side out through the long opening that remains along the side. Insert the bolster pad through this opening. Pin the edges together and slip-stitch by hand with matching thread.

Trio of pincushions
.... *with mix-and-match stripes*

All striped fabrics, from shirting to utilitarian ticking, have great decorative potential. They can be used in patchwork to create interwoven or concentric patterns, and the lines can be embellished with simple embroidery stitches. This trio of pincushions uses all these techniques. The first, inspired by an antique original, is made from a square of fabric. It has gathered corners and is packed hard with stuffing to make the ball-like shape. The second, diamond-shape cushion is made from four smaller squares and it is more lightly filled, while the hexagon pattern on the third is constructed from six triangular patches.

You will need
....

* *10 x 8 inches (25 x 20 cm) each of two different striped fabrics* (fabric A and fabric B) for the round and diamond pincushions

* *20 x 4 inches (50 x 10 cm) striped fabric* for the hexagon pincushion

* *12 x 6 inches (30 x 15 cm) batting* (optional) for the hexagon pincushion

* *Stranded embroidery thread in two colors:* red and blue (we used Sajou Retors du Nord in 2030 red for the round and diamond pincushions, and 2876 agate for the hexagon pincushion)

* *Colored thread* for basting

* *Sewing thread* to match fabric

* *Narrow ribbon* 7/16 inch (11 mm) wide; we used Sajou red Eiffel Tower ribbon for the diamond pincushion and blue Little Bobbins ribbon for the hexagon pincushion

* *One button each,* 3/4-inch (2-cm) in diameter, for the diamond and hexagon pincushions

* *Safety standard polyester fiber filling*

* *Template* on page 177

* *4¾-inch (12-cm) metal pan scourer* (optional) for the hexagon pincushion

* *Basic sewing kit* (see pages 14–16)

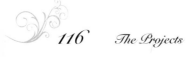

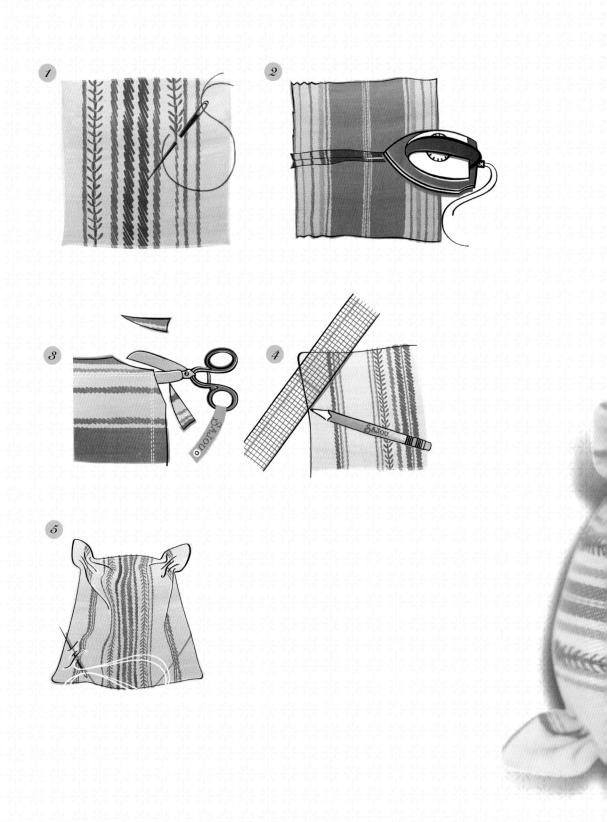

Cutting out

For the round cushion, cut:

* **One 6-inch (15-cm) square from fabric A**
* **Two matching 6 x 3¼-inch (15 x 8-cm) rectangles from fabric B** for the back

For the diamond cushion, cut:

* **Two matching 6¼-inch (8-cm) squares from light fabric A**
* **Two matching 6¼-inch (8-cm) squares and two matching 6 x 3¼-inch (15 x 8-cm) rectangles from dark fabric B** for the back

For the hexagon cushion, cut:

* **Two sets of six matching triangles from fabric A** (see step 1 of project)
* **Two circles of quilt batting, 5½ inches (14 cm) in diameter,** if you are filling the pincushion with a metal pan scourer

Round pincushion

1
Pick out a dominant color from the fabric and select a thread that matches it closely, such as the red used here. Using two strands of the thread, embroider a row of joined fly stitches (see page 35) on each side of the center line, in a vertical row from top to bottom.

2
With right sides facing, pin and baste the two back rectangles together along one long edge, matching up the stripes carefully. Machine stitch, using a ¼-inch (5-mm) seam allowance but leaving a 2-inch (5-cm) gap in the center of the seam. You will turn the pincushion right side out through this space. Press the seam open.

3
Again with right sides facing, pin and baste the front and back together. Machine stitch all the way around the four sides, ⅜ inch (1 cm) from the edge. Reduce the bulk at the corners by trimming an elongated triangle from each side, snipping to within ⅛ inch (3 mm) of the stitch line.

Turn the cushion right side out by easing the fabric through the gap in the center back. Gently push out the corners with the point of a pencil or a knitting needle, then press lightly.

4
Mark the ends of the gathering lines by drawing two points on each edge of the square, 1⅜ inches (3.5 cm) in from the corners. Draw a diagonal pencil line across each corner to join up the two dots.

5
Using a double length of sewing thread, work a line of five or six running stitches along the first line. Pull up tightly to make the "ear" and fasten off the thread securely. Do the same at each corner.

Stuff the cushion by pushing small clumps of polyester filling through the gap. Push it right into the corners and pack it down hard until the cushion is rounded and no more filling can fit in. Pin the two open edges together, then slip-stitch the gap closed.

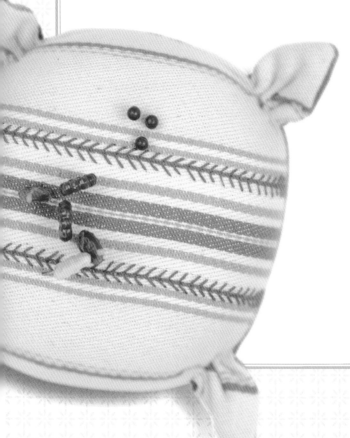

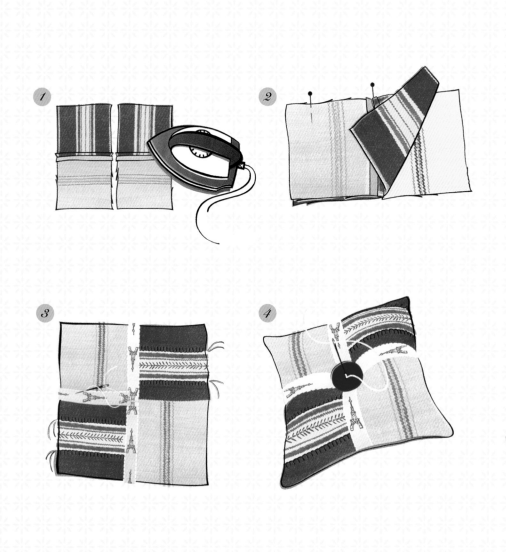

Diamond pincushion
....

1

With right sides facing, pin the 3¼-inch (8-cm) striped squares together in pairs so that the stripes lie at right angles to each other. Machine stitch ¼ inch (5 mm) from the edge and press the seams open.

2

Place the pairs together, with right sides facing, so that the light squares lie against the dark. Insert a pin at the point where the center seams meet up, then pin the rest of the top edge. Machine stitch, using a ¼-inch (5-mm) seam allowance, then press the seam open.

3

Cut four 3¼-inch (8-cm) lengths of ribbon. If it has a distinct pattern, like this Eiffel Tower motif, make sure that all the pieces are identical. Pin and baste the first length of ribbon across the seam between two patches. Slip-stitch in place with matching thread. Sew the other three lengths across the other seams to make a cross.

Make up the pincushion as in steps 2–3 for the round pincushion. Fill it with stuffing, pushing small amounts into the corners with a pencil until they become pointed,

then fill the rest of the pincushion. Pin the two sides of the opening and slip-stitch together.

4

Sew a large button securely to the center of the pincushion, using a long needle to take the thread right through to the back.

Hexagon pincushion

Each side of the cushion is made up of six identical triangular patches, using the template on page 177. The stripes should all run horizontally, so that they create a hexagon when the triangles are stitched together.

1

Position the template on the fabric so that the two bottom corners line up on the same stripe, then draw around the outside edge. Draw another six triangles in the spaces between them, matching these up along a different part of the design. Cut out all the patches.

2

With right sides facing, hold the first two patches together, lining up the stripes carefully. Pin, baste, and then machine stitch the top diagonal edge, using a ¼-inch (5-mm) seam allowance. Press the seam open, then add another patch to make a half circle. Repeat steps 1 and 2 to make another half circle.

3

Match up two half circles with the right sides facing inward. Angle the pins along the stripes, checking that they line up exactly, then machine stitch the center seam. Press the seam allowances open. Make up the pincushion back in the same way, using the second set of six triangles.

4

Using two strands of a contrasting thread, such as the blue used here, work a round of joined fly stitches (see page 35) on the pincushion top. Follow the stripes to create a neat hexagon shape.

5

If you are using a pan scourer to fill the cushion, place a circle of batting over the top of it, then place the cushion top across it. Secure the cushion top and the batting to the scourer, inserting a pin at the end of each seam.

6

Attach the other circle of batting and the cushion bottom to the other half of the scourer, matching up the seam lines carefully. Hand sew the top and bottom together.

Alternatively, the cushion can be made up by simply stitching the top and bottom together, with right sides facing, and leaving a 2-inch (5-cm) gap in the seam. Press back the seam allowance all around, turn right side out, and stuff firmly. Sew up the gap.

7

Thread a long needle with a 24-inch (60-cm) length of the stranded embroidery thread. Take it down at the center of the pincushion, round the outside edge in line with a seam, then back up and through the center. Do this along each seam line, pulling on the thread gently, and fasten off securely at the back.

8

Finish off by pinning a length of ribbon all the way around the outside edge to cover the seam line. Leave a ⅜-inch (1-cm) overlap at the ends, tuck under the first ¼ inch (5 mm) and slip-stitch down the top and bottom edges of the ribbon. Sew a large button securely to the center of the pincushion, using a long needle to take the thread right through to the back.

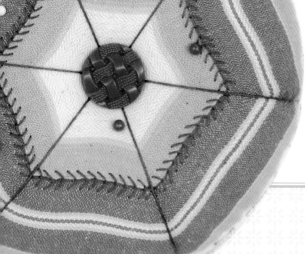

LAINE S.ᵗᵉ PIERRE

LILLE France
Fabrication française
Ets TOULEMONDE   Successeurs

50 % laine
50 % polyamide
LES LAINES
MARQUE S.ᵗᵉPIERRE
sont recommandées
pour tous les travaux de Dames
coloris
603
REPRISER BRODER FESTONNER

TRIO OF PINCUSIONS
pages 116–125

Join striped patches to
create new patterns

I love this
Sajou
ribbon!

Woven
ticking for a
red, white, and
blue color scheme

Use two strands
of thread that
show up well

Fly stitch in a contrasting
color worked along the stripes

Pearl buttons add
highlights

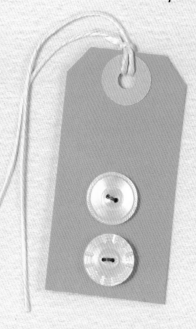

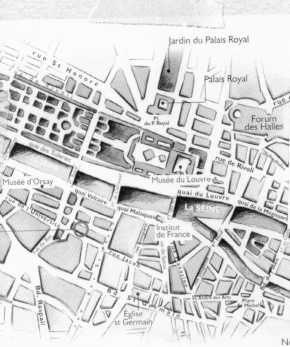

Jardin du Palais Royal

rue St Honoré

Palais Royal

Pl.
du P. Royal

Forum
des Halles

rue de Rivoli

quai des Tuileries

Musée d'Orsay

rue de l'Université

Musée du Louvre

quai Voltaire
quai Malaquais

quai du Louvre
quai de la Mégisserie

La SEINE

Institut
de France

Bd. Raspail

rue Jacob

rue St André des Arts

Place
St Michel

Eglise
st Germain

LE SEINE

Notre Dame de Paris

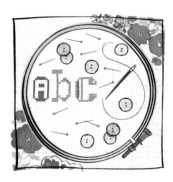

Sampler cushion

.... *with mismatched alphabets*

Generations of young girls have learned to sew by working cross-stitch samplers, carefully copying their letters and numbers from printed charts. This small cushion cover gives a new twist to traditional needlework techniques by randomly mismatching letters from five different alphabets. These were found in pattern books that date from the 1930s and all of them have a distinctively Art Deco look, evocative of that era. The lower-case alphabet was designed in imitation of an old-fashioned typewriter font, while those set within circles recall typewriter keys.

Finished size
....
12 x 8 inches (30 x 20 cm)

You will need
....

* *20 x 10 inches (50 x 25 cm) furnishing fabric;* allow more if you want to match up the two sides
* *Chart* on page 176
* *16 x 12 inches (40 x 30 cm) off-white 32-count linen*
* *Stranded embroidery thread* in three colors: wine red, dark coral, and dusky pink (we used Sajou Retors du Nord in 2409 bordeaux; 2033 gladiola; and 2469 rosewood)
* *12½ x 8¾ inches (32 x 22 cm) white cotton fabric*
* *Iron-on hemming tape*
* *Stranded embroidery thread* to match the furnishing fabric
* *Five buttons*, ½ inch (12 mm) in diameter
* *48 inches (120 cm) fine flanged piping cord*
* *Colored thread* for basting
* *12 x 8-inch (30 x 20-cm) cushion pad*
* *Basic sewing kit* (see pages 14–16)

Petit-point key fobs

.... *in Scotch and tent stitch*

The spare keys for your home or car will never go astray if you keep them safely attached to a specially made fob and hang them up in a safe place. This charted design—inspired by an antique steel key that once locked an imposing front door—is stitched in fine wool onto 18-count canvas. There are two variations on the theme, one sewn in simple tent stitch throughout and the other in a combination of tent stitch and textured Scotch stitch. If you prefer cross-stitch, the key motif alone would work well in stranded cotton on a background of colored linen.

Finished size
....
4¾ x 2¾ inches (12 x 7 cm), plus ring

You will need
....
FOR EACH KEY FOB:

* *10 x 8-inch (25 x 20-cm) 18-count canvas*
* *Templates on page 178*
* *6 x 4-inch (15 x 10-cm) medium-weight cardboard*
* *6 x 4-inch (15 x 10-cm) black cotton fabric* for the backing
* *Sewing thread* to match binding
* *Split ring*, 1¼ inches (3 cm) in diameter
* *Masking tape*
* *10 x 8-inch (25 x 20-cm) wooden stretcher frame*
* *Thumbtacks*
* *Glue stick*
* *Basic sewing kit* (see pages 14–16)

FOR THE SCOTCH-STITCH FOB:

* *Fine stranded wool* yarn in four colors: mustard, gold, mid-gray, and cream (we used Sajou Laine Saint-Pierre in 422 mustard; 360 gold; 126 dust; and 104 cream)
* *20 inches (50 cm) narrow black bias binding*

FOR THE TENT-STITCH FOB:

* *Fine stranded wool* yarn in three colors: light gray, gold, and slate gray (we used Sajou Laine Saint-Pierre in 118 kaolin; 360 gold; and 914 slate)
* *20 inches (50 cm) narrow gold bias binding*

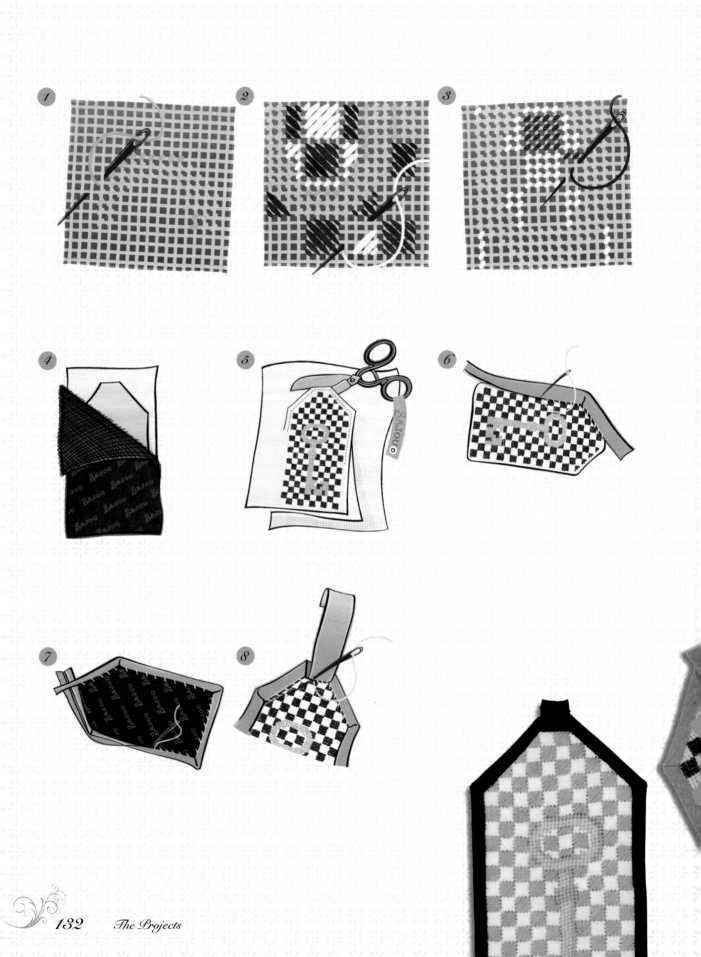

Preparing the canvas

Fold the canvas in half lengthwise and then widthwise. Lightly draw over the fold lines with a pencil to mark the center. Bind the edges of the canvas with masking tape to stop the yarn from snagging, then secure the canvas to the frame with thumbtacks.

Scotch-stitch key fob

1

Work the key in tent stitch (see page 27) using a fine tapestry needle. Each square on the chart represents a single stitch. Embroider the main part of the key in mustard, positioning the stitch that is at the center of the chart in the center of the canvas. Add the darker shaded areas in gold yarn.

2

Work the background in Scotch stitch (see page 27)—small squares of seven graded diagonal stitches. Each Scotch stitch is represented by one of the 4 x 4-square blocks on the chart. First, work the mid-gray cushions in diagonal rows, from bottom left to top right. You will need to alter the length of the stitches where the blocks are overlapped by the key. Then fill in the cream cushions, stitching from right to left.

Tent-stitch key fob

3

Each square on this chart represents a single tent stitch. Start by embroidering the key in gold, working the stitch that is at the center of the chart in the center of the canvas. Sew all the light squares of the checkerboard in light gray yarn, then fill in the dark squares in slate gray.

Making up the fobs

4

Trace or photocopy the key fob outline on page 178 and cut out this shape from cardboard. Using a glue stick, lightly coat the back of the completed stitches lightly with glue. Press the cardboard template on top, lining up the edges carefully. Add another light layer of glue and stick the backing fabric, right side up, over the cardboard and canvas. Place a heavy book on top and let dry.

5

Stitch the three layers together, $\frac{1}{16}$ inch (2 mm) from the stitches, by hand or machine. Trim away the surplus canvas and fabric so that there is a $\frac{1}{8}$-inch (3-mm) margin all the way around the embroidered area.

TIP

If you're using Sajou Laine Saint-Pierre, use four strands; if you're using another yarn, use two or three strands, depending on the ply.

6

Starting at the bottom diagonal edge and leaving a $\frac{3}{4}$-inch (2-cm) overlap, position the folded edge of the bias binding close to the outside edge of the stitches on the cut edge of the fob. Sew it in place with matching thread, making a row of tiny stitches through the canvas and the backing fabric. Fold the binding at an angle so that it fits neatly around the corners.

7

When you have reached the second diagonal edge, turn the fob over. Fold over the other edge of the binding so that it conceals the raw edges and slip-stitch it to the backing fabric.

8

Trim the ends of the binding in line with the top edge. Cut a 2-inch (5-cm) length from the remaining binding and press under a $\frac{3}{8}$-inch (1-cm) turning at each end. Sew one folded end securely to the back of the fob, covering the cut ends. Slip on the split ring, then sew the other fold to the front. Stitch the front and back of the loop together to keep the ring firmly in place.

TIP

You may prefer to work without a frame, in which case the canvas may distort slightly because of the diagonal stitches. If this happens, you will need to block the finished piece to straighten it out. See how to do this on page 27, along with details of how to work tent and Scotch stitch.

Lavender hearts

.... *with flower-embroidered trim*

Hearts have a universal appeal as a symbol of love and affection, so this pair of embroidered versions would make a perfect small gift for your best friend or a family member. Both practical and pretty, they are embroidered with a floral band, trimmed with crisp white lace, and filled with dried lavender flowers. Hang them up in a closet or wardrobe, or keep them in a bedroom drawer, to add subtle fragrance to your clothes and to ward off any visiting moths.

Finished size
....
4¾ x 6 inches (12 x 15 cm)

You will need
....

FOR EACH HEART:

* *Stranded embroidery thread* in two colors: apple green and fuchsia pink (we used Sajou Retors du Nord in 2019 spring and 2026 fuchsia)

* *12 inches (30 cm) lace edging;* we used Sajou guipure lace No 9

* *Sewing thread* to match fabric

* *Templates* on page 179

* *1½ ounces (40 g) dried lavender*

* *12 inches (30 cm) pink cord or string*

* *Basic sewing kit* (see pages 14–16)

FOR THE WHITE HEART:

* *6 x 10 inches (15 x 25 cm) white cotton fabric*

* *6 x 10 inches (15 x 25 cm) pink polka-dot cotton fabric*

* *Template* on page 179

FOR THE PINK HEART:

* *12 x 8 inches (30 x 20 cm) pink polka-dot cotton fabric*

* *6 x 1⅜-inch (15 x 3.5-cm) strip of white cotton fabric*

* *Template* on page 179

Cutting out

FOR THE WHITE HEART, CUT:

* *From white cotton, cut two 6 x 4-inch (15 x 10-cm) rectangles for the front and a 6 x 1-inch (15 x 2.5-cm) strip for the embroidery*
* *From pink cotton, cut two 6 x ¾-inch (15 x 2-cm) strips for the front and two 6 x 4-inch (15 x 10-cm) rectangles for the back*

FOR THE PINK HEART, CUT:

* *From pink cotton, cut four 6 x 4-inch (15 x 10-cm) rectangles;* two for the front and two for the back

White heart front

1

With the right side facing inward, pin a pink strip to the white strip for the embroidery. Machine stitch together ¼ inch (6 mm) from the edge, then press the seam allowance toward the pink fabric. Join the second pink strip to the other side of the white strip in the same way. Pin and stitch the two white rectangles to the outside edges of the pink strips and then press both seams toward the pink fabric.

2

Following the instructions on page 24, transfer the template outline onto the white strip. Embroider the motif, using two strands of thread throughout; details of how to work all the stitches are on pages 28–35. Using apple green thread, work small backstitches along the curving lines. Work a single lazy daisy stitch over each short straight line, extending these over the edges of pink fabric.

3

Using fuchsia pink thread, embroider the dots in raised satin stitch. Start by filling in the circle with parallel straight stitches, then stitch over them in the opposite direction.

4

Cut the lace edging in half. Position one length along the top edge of the pink strip, making sure that you center the point over the middle dot. Pin in place if you want. Using white sewing thread, hand stitch the bottom edge of the lace to the white fabric with small overcast stitches. Sew the other length of lace to the bottom edge, matching up the points.

Pink heart front

With right sides together, pin a pink rectangle to each long edge of the narrow white strip. Using a ¼-inch (6-mm) seam allowance, machine stitch. Press the seams toward the pink fabric. Transfer the second template to the white band and embroider the stems, leaves, and dots as for the white heart. Hand sew the lace, as in step 4.

Assembling the hearts

5

The backs of both hearts are made in the same way. With right sides facing, pin together the long edges of the two pink rectangles for the back. Using a ⅜-inch (1-cm) seam, machine stitch, leaving a 2-inch (5-cm) gap at the center. Press the seam open.

6

Trace or photocopy the full-size heart template from page 179 and cut out. Place the completed heart front, right side down, and position the template on top, lining up the horizontal guideline with the top seam line. Pin it in place, then draw around the outside edge with an air-erasable pen or a pencil.

7

With right sides facing, pin the front and back of the heart together. Machine stitch slowly and carefully along the pencil outline. Trim the seam allowance down to ⅛ inch (3 mm). Cut a tiny notch at the top, between the two curves, being careful not to cut through the stitching.

Turn the heart right side out by pushing the fabric through the gap in the center back. Insert a knitting needle through the gap and use the point to gently ease out the seams. Press lightly.

8

Stuff the heart with lavender, one spoonful at a time. Push it right down to the point and up into the curves. When the heart is plump and full, close the gap by hand with ladder stitch.

Tie the two ends of the cord or string together to make a loop. Hand stitch securely to the top of the heart, between the two curves.

Country kitchen tray cloth

.... *with drawn threadwork edging*

Traditional drawn threadwork edging gives a polished finish to any project and is surprisingly easy to do. The scattered French-style kitchen motifs on this tray cloth—coffeepots, croissants, canisters, and plates—are embroidered in different stitches but are also simple, and they can be arranged as densely or as sparsely as you want. For our version, we've lined up the motifs in rows, but if you prefer a more random approach, you could angle the motifs and spread them more thinly. You can also use the same drawn threadwork technique as a decorative border for a square napkin and stitch a single motif in one corner.

You will need

* **32-count blue embroidery linen,** 1 ¼ inches (3 cm) larger all around than the intended size of your finished cloth or napkin

* **Sewing thread** to match linen

* **Colored thread** for basting

* **Stranded embroidery thread** in eight colors: white, turquoise, grass green, red, fawn, honey brown, dark blue, and mid-blue (we used Sajou Retors du Nord in 2003 pure white; 2010 azure; 2014 jardin; 2032 andrinople; 2266 deer; 2570 honey brown; 2682 sapphire; and 2876 agate)

* **Templates** on pages 180–181

* **Basic sewing kit** (see pages 14–16)

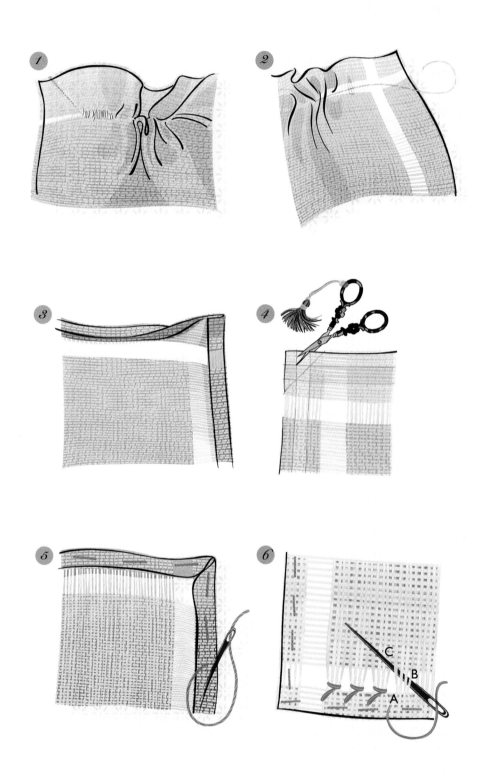

Making the tray cloth

1

Start by pulling out the threads for the drawn threadwork. Measure 1 inch (2.5 cm) down from the center of the top edge and use a tapestry needle to pull up one of the horizontal threads from the fabric. Draw the thread out to one side edge, gathering the fabric and slowly and evenly pulling the thread out of the weave.

2

Working downward from the first thread, pull out nine more horizontal threads. Repeat the process on the other three sides of the fabric. This will leave you with small square holes at each corner where the "stripes" of removed thread cross each other.

3

Fold each edge of your linen firmly down ³/₈ inch (1 cm) from the edge, pressing with your fingers to form a crease, then turn again to make a double hem. (You can press the hem with an iron, but a finger crease works as well.) The inside edge of the hem should lie along the edge of the "stripe" of drawn threads. Unfold the creases.

4

Now miter the corners. Fold and press each corner diagonally inward so that the outside edges line up with the "stripes" of drawn threads. Trim off the outside corners outside the crease line where shown to reduce the bulk of fabric. Slip-stitch the short diagonal edges together.

5

Refold the corners along the diagonal creases, then refold the double hems along the side edges. Using a contrasting sewing thread, baste the hem down around all four sides of the cloth with large running stitches.

6

It's time to "draw" the threads together with single hem stitch. Thread a needle with sewing thread to match the linen. With the wrong side of the fabric facing you, and working from just inside the square hole at the bottom left corner, bring the needle up through the folded hem at A. Slide the needle under four threads to the right, from B to C.

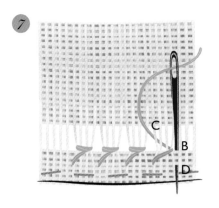

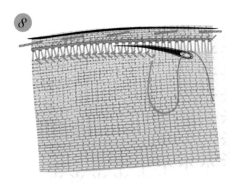

C
B
D

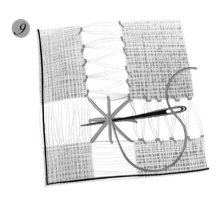

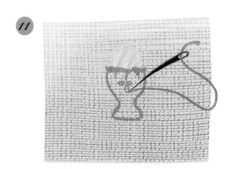

7

For the second stage of the stitch, take the needle back between the vertical threads at B and pull it out through the double hem at D. Repeat these two steps all the way to the square hole at the bottom right corner.

8

Turn the linen the other way and work as in step 6 along the opposite side of the same stripe, this time sliding the needle under two threads from each group of drawn threads. This will pull the drawn threads crosswise to create a zigzag effect.

9

Work four star stitches (see page 34) to stabilize the corners of the cloth. Make two diagonal stitches from corner to corner of the square hole, then two more from side to side. Weave your needle in and out of the stitches at the center to pull them together and fasten off (see photo on right).

10

Following the instructions on page 24, photocopy or trace the 20 breakfast motifs from the templates on pages 180–181. Cut them out and arrange them on your cloth, adjusting the layout to fit the proportions. (Follow our layout on page 144–145 or design your own arrangement.) Draw around each one with a sharp pencil or air-erasable marking pen, then add in the details.

11

The motifs are worked in a variety of stitches, using two strands of thread throughout. You can use the same stitches as we did or vary them as you want. You can find details of how to work all the stitches on pages 28–35.

Stitch guide

Row one, from left:

Tureen
Outline in turquoise stem stitch; borders and handles in white satin stitch; triangles in turquoise satin stitch; dots in red French knots.

Plate
Outline in closely spaced red blanket stitch; cherries in red satin stitch; leaves in grass green satin stitch.

Cup and saucer
Outline in mid-blue stem stitch; stripes in dark blue-and-white satin stitch.

Coffeepot
Outline and stripes in turquoise stem stitch; knob and handle in turquoise satin stitch; inner border in fawn backstitch; dots in fawn French knots.

Egg cup
Egg in honey brown raised satin stitch; cup outline in red stem stitch; rim in red satin stitch; flower in red lazy daisy stitch.

Row two, from left:

Egg cup
Egg in fawn raised satin stitch; cup outline in mid-blue stem stitch; rim in mid-blue satin stitch; flower in mid-blue lazy daisy stitch.

Pitcher
Outline in grass green stem stitch; handle in grass green satin stitch; center band in red satin stitch with back stitch outline; ovals in grass green lazy daisy stitches.

Canister
Outline in white stem stitch; knob and squares in mid-blue satin stitch; dots in red French knots.

Coffee bowl
Outline in red stem stitch; rim in mid-blue satin stitch and red straight stitch; flowers in red lazy daisy stitch; leaves in grass green lazy daisy stitch.

Pitcher
Outline in mid-blue stem stitch; rim and handle in mid-blue satin stitch; leaves in grass green satin stitch; stems in grass green backstitch; cherries in red satin stitch.

Row three, from left:

Croissant
Outline in honey brown stem stitch.

Coffeepot
Outline in red stem stitch; knob and handle in red satin stitch; checker squares in red-and-white satin stitch.

Sugar bowl
Outline in mid-blue stem stitch; border in turquoise satin stitch; flowers in red lazy daisy stitch; flower centers in fawn with French knots.

Coffee grinder
Outline in red stem stitch, infilled with red satin stitch; handle in mid-blue satin stitch outlined with backstitch; label in dark blue satin stitch outlined with back stitch.

Cup and saucer
Cup in red-and-white satin stitch with a red satin stitch handle; saucer in white satin stitch.

Row four, from left:

Cup and saucer
Outline in turquoise stem stitch; stripes in turquoise satin stitch; fine stripes in fawn backstitch; dots in fawn French knots.

Coffee bowl
Outline in mid-blue stem stitch; rim in mid-blue satin stitch; leaves in grass green lazy daisy stitch; flowers in red lazy daisy stitch.

Pitcher
Outline in white stem stitch; handle in white satin stitch with backstitch outline; stripes in red-and-white satin stitch.

Croissant
Outline in honey brown stem stitch.

Canister
Outline in dark blue stem stitch; knob in dark blue satin stitch; checker stripes in white-and-dark blue satin stitch.

Running rabbit cushion

.... *with patchwork border*

This bounding wild rabbit shows how the most basic embroidery stitch—a simple straight stitch—can be used to build up a complex image, in the same way that an artist creates a painting from a series of individual brush strokes. It is worked in three shades of brown plus a soft off-white to create a shaded, three-dimensional look, with pink and golden thread for the ear and eye. Simple patchwork borders, in bright citrus colors to complement the naturalistic fur shades, frame the motif at top and bottom.

You will need

* **40 x 20-inch (100 x 50-cm) rectangle of furniture-weight off-white cotton or linen fabric**
* **Four 14 x 4-inch (35 x 10-cm) pieces of cotton fabric** (we used fawn, orange, lilac, and lemon)
* **Template** on page 182
* **Stranded embroidery thread** in nine colors: dark brown, mid-brown, off-white, light brown, shell pink, old gold, yellow-green, olive and orange (we used Sajou Retors du Nord in 2332 auburn; 2234 chamois; 2000 undyed; 2266 deer; 2018 baby pink; 2549 autumn; 2034 mousse; 2445 olive; and 2405 orange)
* **Cream sewing thread**
* **One 8 x 2½-inch (20 x 6-cm) strip of green cotton fabric**
* **Sewing or embroidery threads** to match border fabrics
* **Colored thread** for basting
* **10–15 small pearl buttons**
* **16-inch (40-cm) square cushion pad**
* **Basic sewing kit** (see pages 14–16)

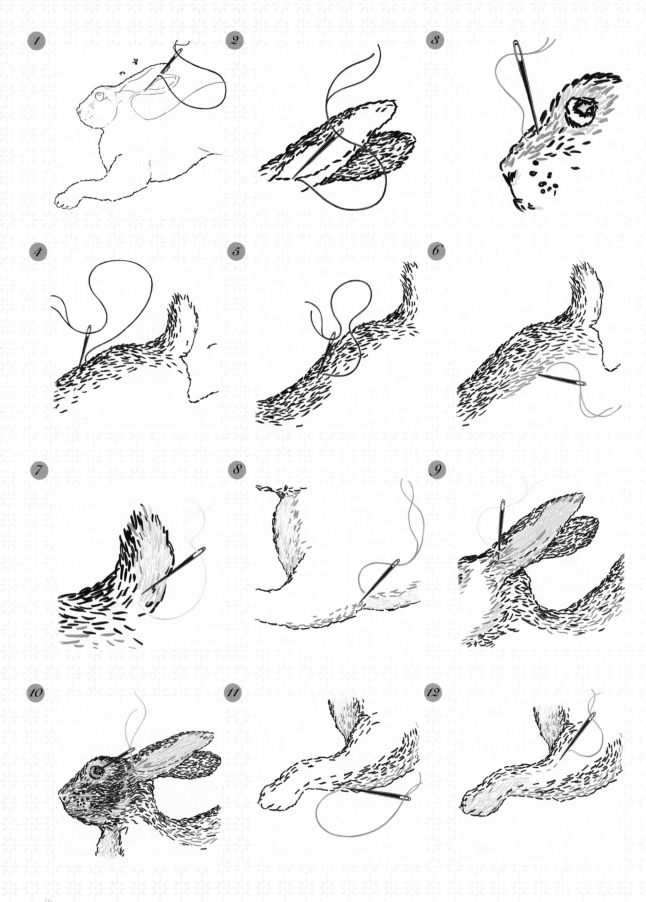

Cutting out

FROM THE OFF-WHITE COTTON, CUT:

* **One 16-inch (40-cm) square** for the front panel
* **Two 10 x 16-inch (25 x 40-cm) rectangles** for the back panels

FROM THE FOUR COLORED COTTON FABRICS, CUT:

* **Eight 2½ x 3¼-inch (6 x 8-cm) rectangles**
* **Six 2½-inch (6-cm) squares**

Embroidering the rabbit

Trace or photocopy the rabbit template on page 182 and transfer the shape to the front panel, positioning it so that the front paw lies 4 inches (10 cm) in from the left edge and 4¾ inches (12 cm) up from the bottom edge (see page 24).

1
Mount the fabric in an embroidery hoop, then work the motifs as instructed below, using two strands of thread throughout; you can find details of how to work all the stitches on pages 28–35. Start by embroidering over the rabbit's outline in dark brown backstitch. Make the stitches different lengths to give a looser, more "sketched" look to the line.

2
Still using dark brown thread, work a few extra short stitches around the edge of the back ear, then fill in the shape with small straight stitches in mid-brown, following the direction of the outline. Add

extra dark brown stitches to the top edge of the front ear, then fill in the outline with mid-brown.

3
Define the features with dark brown thread: fill in the eye with satin stitch, work the nose in straight stitch, and embroider the dots with French knots. Add a few straight stitches along the top of the head and between the eye and dots. Work a round of straight stitches around the eye with off-white thread, then work two straight stitches to highlight. Using light brown thread, sew more straight stitches around the eye, varying the length, then work more light brown across the snout.

4
Shade in the rabbit's back and the top of the tail with a ⅜-inch (1-cm) band of dark brown straight stitches, working them parallel to the outline. Space them closer together toward the outside edge.

5
Change to mid-brown thread and continue filling in with short straight stitches, working them in between the darker ones.

6
Work light brown stitches around the tip of the tail and across the rump, angling them in a soft curve to give shape to the hind leg.

7
Fill in the tail with off-white straight stitches, overlapping them to create a dense, furry look.

8
Fill in the chest and belly with off-white stitches, angling them to give form to the body. Work a scattering of light brown stitches along the inside edge of each off-white patch.

9
With dark brown thread, work the shading across the neck, then add off-white and light brown stitches to define the inside edge of the head. Fill in the ear with overlapping shell pink stitches and add light brown stitches at the top and inside edges. Finish off with a few off-white stitches inside the dark brown outline.

10
Add more off-white stitches around the nose and cheek, then indicate the cheek outline with dark brown stitches. Complete the rabbit's head with mid-brown stitches, angling them to create a three-dimensional look. Fill in the eye with a single strand of old gold thread.

11
Work lines of short light brown stitches inside the "elbow" outline to give the front leg form. Work mid-brown and then dark brown stitches inside these, and add more dark brown stitches along the upper edge.

12
Fill in the lower part of the leg and paw with closely spaced off-white stitches and define the toes with dark brown straight stitches. Work light brown straight stitches on each side of the white block, taking them right up to the top of the leg.

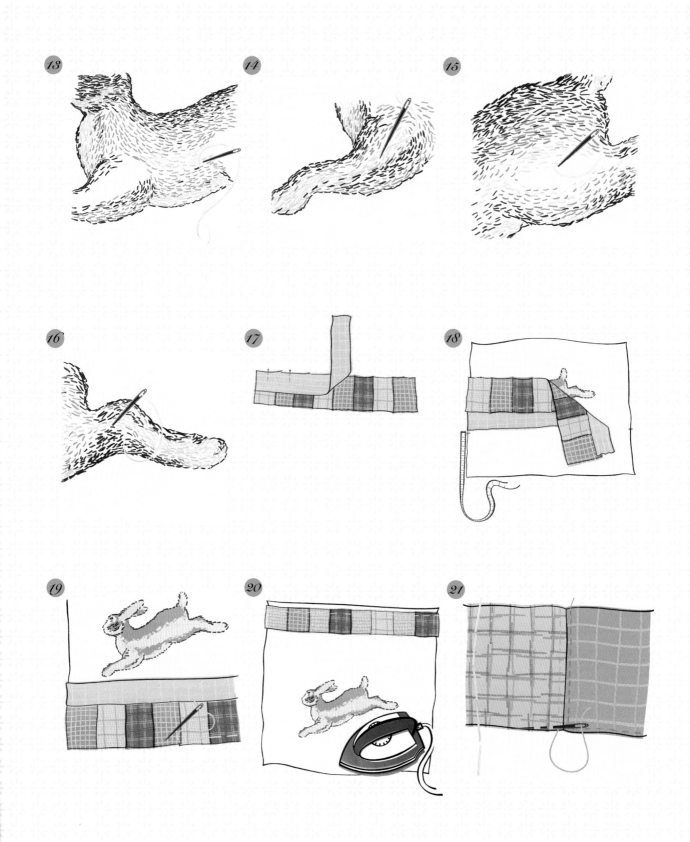

13

Start shading the trunk and chest by adding more light brown stitches in line with the back and belly, then fill in the center part with off-white. Angle these stitches as shown.

14

Complete the front leg by working a curved line of mid-brown stitches at the point where it meets the trunk. Shade it in with concentric light brown and off-white stitches, following the curves to give a rounded look. Add more stitches to the chest.

15

Give a rounded look to the thigh by working two curved bands of straight stitches in light brown. Add a scattering of mid-brown stitches across them and a few extra dark brown lowlights at the outside edges. Fill in the center with off-white.

16

Finish off the back leg by shading the edges with dark brown where shown, then working inward, add mid-brown and light brown stitches. Fill in the paw in off-white and embroider dark stitches to divide the toes. Finally, continue the off-white stitches up to the top of the leg.

17
• • •

With right sides together, using a ¼-inch (6-mm) seam allowance, join the eight colored cotton rectangles together along their long sides to make the bottom border strip. Press all the seams to one side. Pin and stitch the green strip to the top edge with right sides together, then press the seam allowances toward the patchwork.

18
• • •

Mark two points on the two side edges of the front panel, 4¼ inches (10.5 cm) up from the bottom edge. With right sides together, place the top edge of the bottom border strip across the front panel so that the two green corners lie at these points. Pin in place, then machine stitch ¼ inch (6 mm) from the edge.

19

Fold the border back over the front panel and press it in place. Baste the border panel to the front panel along the side and bottom edges.

20

To make the top border, join the eight colored cotton squares in a row and press the seams to one side. Mark two points 2¼ inches (5.5 cm) down from the top corners of the front panel, then pin the top corners of the border to these points, with right sides together as before. Machine stitch, using a ¼-inch (6-mm) seam allowance, then fold the border back, press in place, and baste to the front panel along the side and bottom edges.

21

Using sewing thread or a single strand of embroidery thread in colors to match each fabric, sew a line of small running stitches along the top and bottom edges of the green strip and around the inside edge of each colored patch.

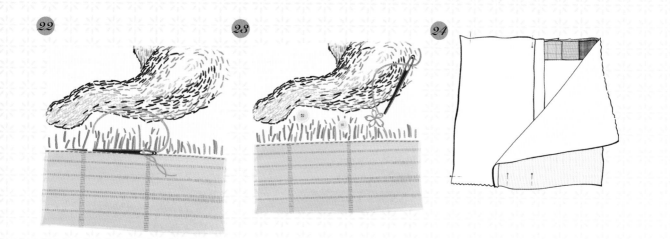

22

Now add the swath of green grass across the left of the cushion front and along the bottom border. The blades are worked with short straight stitches set at various angles. To give depth to the color, those nearest the top are in two strands of yellow-green thread and those along the border are in two shades of olive. Use one strand of each for some of the stitches.

23

Sew the buttons randomly across the grass, using two strands of orange or olive thread. Add a scattering of small orange flowers through the grass, each made up of five lazy daisy stitches.

24

Make a ⅝-inch (1.5-cm) double hem at one long edge of each back panel. With right sides facing and aligning the raw edges, pin one panel to the left edge of the cushion front. Pin the other panel to the right edge. Machine stitch around all four sides, ⅜ inch (1 cm) from the edge. Clip the corners (see page 22) and turn the cover right side out. Ease out the corners and the seams, then press lightly. Insert the cushion pad.

Wild strawberry book cover

.... *with antique herbal embroidery*

A hand-stitched cover turns any plain notebook into something special. This strawberry plant motif, inspired by the engravings in antique herbals, is embroidered onto linen using the simplest of stitches. It would work well for a plain sketchbook or keepsake album, but you could use a check linen dish towel with café motifs for a collection of recipes, for example, or a cross-stitch monogram from the alphabet on page 86 for a personal diary. You could also make a cover for a treasured volume of poems or a favorite hardback novel, as a perfect gift for a friend or family member.

You will need
....
* *Hardback notebook*
* *32-count embroidery linen* in mustard
* *Thin quilt batting*
* *Strawberry plant template* on page 183
* *Stranded embroidery thread* in four colors: yellow, white, black, and red (we used Sajou Retors du Nord in 2038 nankin; 2004 off-white; 2005 black; and 2030 red)
* *Sewing thread* to match fabric
* *Colored thread* for basting
* *Glue stick*
* *Basic sewing kit* (see pages 14–16)

Cutting out

FROM LINEN, CUT:
One rectangle, four times the width of the front cover plus the width of the spine by the height of the notebook plus 1½ inches (4 cm)

FROM BATTING, CUT:
One rectangle, twice the width of the front cover plus the width of the spine by the height of the notebook

The template is 4¾ x 6¾ inches (12 x 17 cm), and can fit neatly in a 5 x 7-inch (13 x 18-cm) cover. The size can be easily adjusted to fit a notebook in a different size.

Working the embroidery

1

Trace or photocopy the template from page 183 (see page 20). Mark the center top and bottom edges of the linen with pins. Wrap the linen around the book so that these points lie midway along the spine and there is a ¾-inch (2-cm) overhang at top and bottom. Position the template centered over the front cover and pin it in place.

Slip a rectangle of dressmaker's carbon paper underneath the template and draw carefully over the outline with a ball-point pen to transfer it onto the linen.

2

Embroider the motifs as instructed below, using two strands of thread throughout unless otherwise indicated; you can find details of how to work all the stitches on pages 28–35. Start off by working a small circle of yellow French knots in the centers of the two open flowers.

3

Using white thread, fill the petals of each strawberry flower and the buds with satin stitch.

4

Sew over the flower outlines with small black backstitches, working close to the petals.

5

Outline the strawberries in red backstitch. Fill them in with short straight stitches, following the contours of the outline. Using just a single strand of thread, sew a few short straight red and yellow stitches over the red filling for the seeds.

6

Work the tops of the strawberries, the stems, and the tendrils in black backstitch, then sew over the leaf outlines, veins, and tendrils. Finish off by adding the shaded areas in straight stitch. Press the finished work lightly from the wrong side.

Making up the cover

Apply a light layer of adhesive from the glue stick to the front and back covers of the notebook, plus the spine, and glue the batting down.

7

Press under a ⅝-inch (1.5-cm) turning along each short end of the linen cover. With the right side facing downward, wrap the fabric around the notebook. Fold the neatened ends inside the covers, making sure that the flaps are equal in length. Pin together at the top and bottom of each cover, then baste close to the edges. Carefully remove from the notebook and machine stitch along both basted lines, stitching straight across the spine.

8

Trim a small triangle from each corner to reduce the bulk, then press the two seam allowances to the front and back respectively. Turn the cover right side out. Bend back the covers of the book and slide them into the flaps.

I love these cute little strawberry stickers

The first strawberries of spring in the garden at Versailles

Strawberries have such a rich color

Use two strands of thread on 32 – count embroidery linen

Fraisier à Bouquets.

P. J. Redouté — 103.

Fragaria.

Chapuis.

WILD
STRAWBERRY
BOOK COVER
pages 154–159

Introduction

On the following pages you will find the templates and charts needed to stitch the projects. The free embroidery designs are printed as full-size drawings, so all you will need to do is to make photocopies or draw over the outlines with a sharp pencil on to a sheet of tracing paper. You can find out how to transfer these outlines on to your background fabric on page 24 of the Techniques section. Each colored square on the cross-stitch and needlepoint charts represents a single stitch: the adjacent keys tell you the name of the thread that corresponds to each color. The monogram alphabet is shown in black only so that you can choose your own thread colors.

Vegetable napkins

Page 38

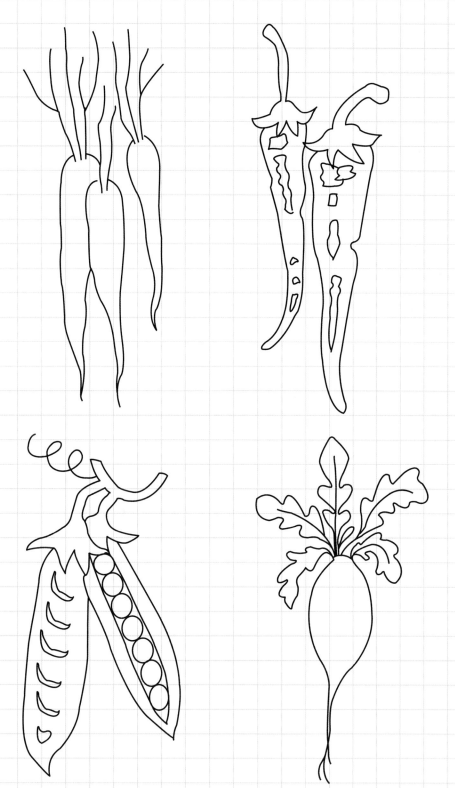

Summer tote bag

Page 46

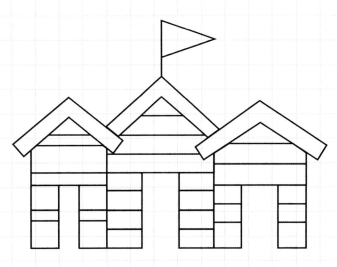

Yacht

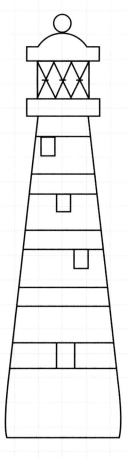

Lighthouse

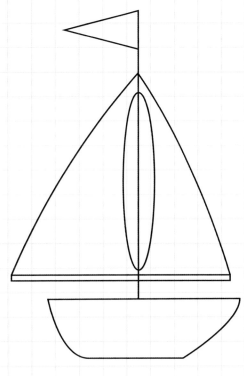

Beach huts

Dandelion crib sheet

Page 66

Anchor

Starfish

Shell

Butterfly collection

Page 72

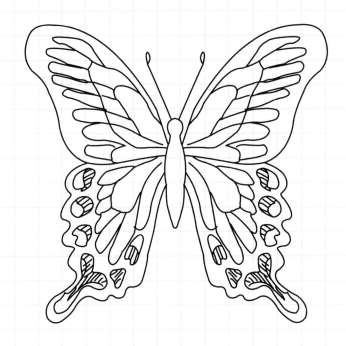

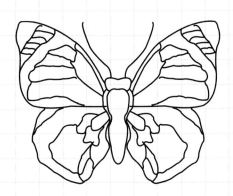

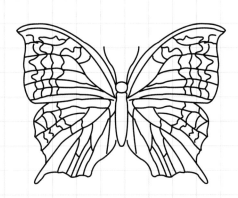

Provençal tablecloth

Page 62

Portable pencil holder

Page 58

Picture sewing tidy

Page 80

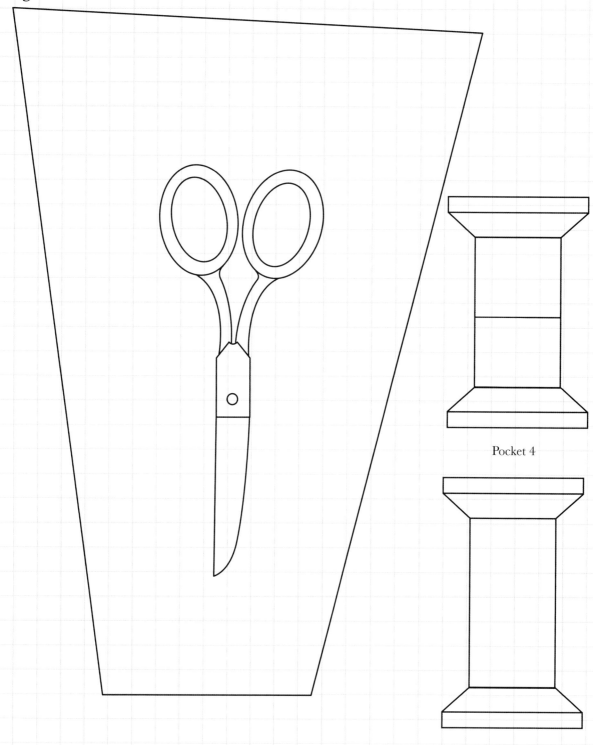

Large shears

Pocket 4

Pocket 5

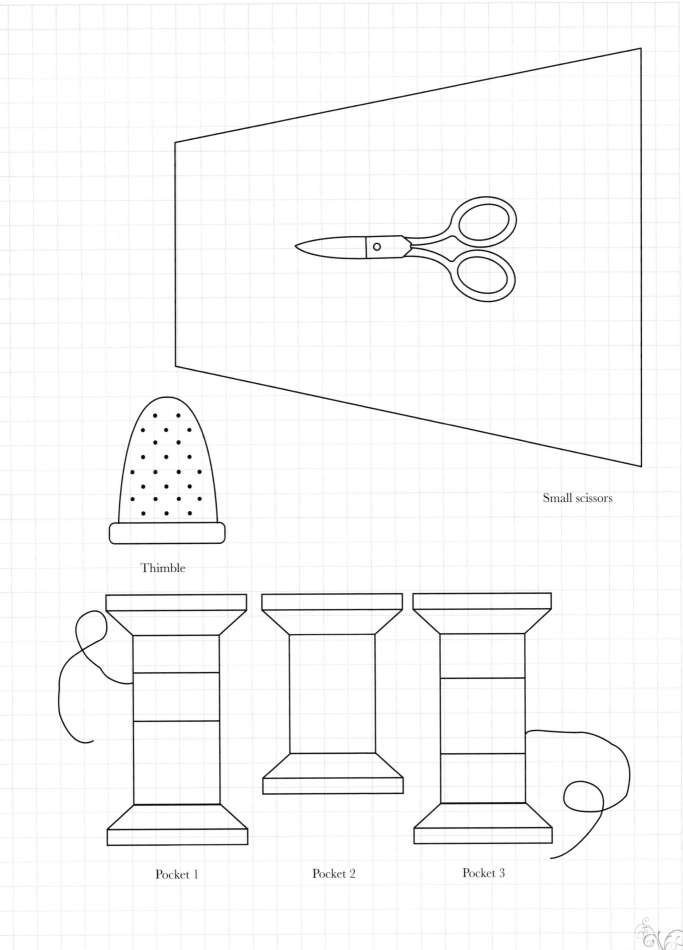

Small scissors

Thimble

Pocket 1

Pocket 2

Pocket 3

Monogrammed sachets

Page 86

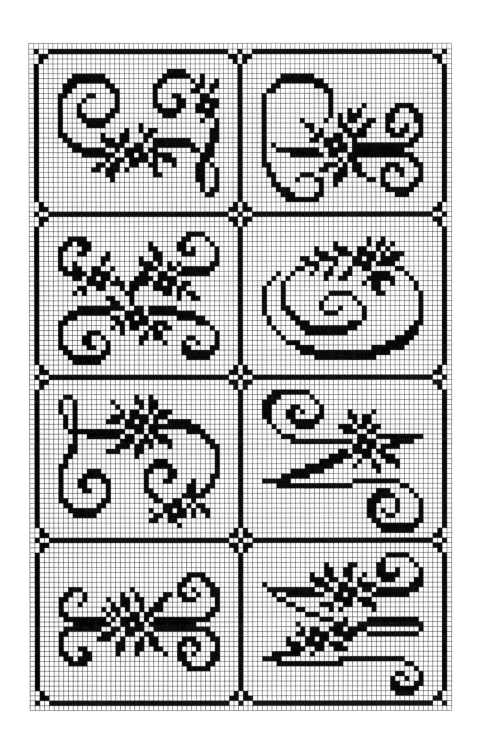

Monogrammed sachets

Silk slipper bag

Page 96

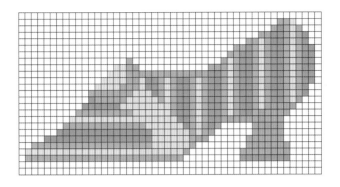

green-yellow / Sajou Retors du Nord in 2034 moss
dusky pink / Sajou Retors du Nord in 2469 rosewood
shell pink / Sajou Retors du Nord in 2535 blush
medium turquoise / Sajou Retors du Nord in 2777 emerald

Twenties clutch bag

Page 52

emerald blue / Sajou Tonkin in 1017 emerald
palest blue / Sajou Tonkin in 1011 sky blue
dark blue / Sajou Retors du Nord in 2964 navy

Petit-point key fobs

Page 130

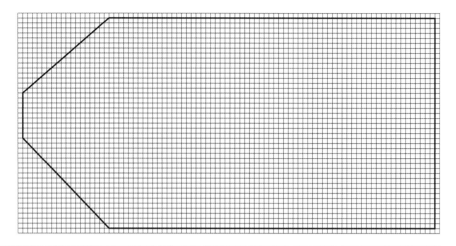

Tent-stitch fob   Scotch-stitch fob

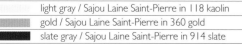

	light gray / Sajou Laine Saint-Pierre in 118 kaolin
	gold / Sajou Laine Saint-Pierre in 360 gold
	slate gray / Sajou Laine Saint-Pierre in 914 slate

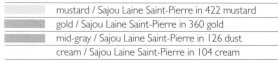

	mustard / Sajou Laine Saint-Pierre in 422 mustard
	gold / Sajou Laine Saint-Pierre in 360 gold
	mid-gray / Sajou Laine Saint-Pierre in 126 dust
	cream / Sajou Laine Saint-Pierre in 104 cream

Lavender hearts

Page 134

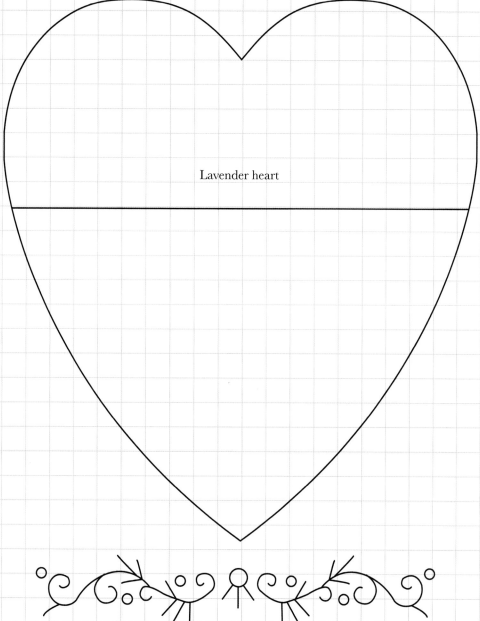

Lavender heart

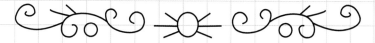

White heart

Pink heart

Country kitchen tray cloth

Page 138

Row 1

Row 2

Row 3

Row 4

Running rabbit cushion

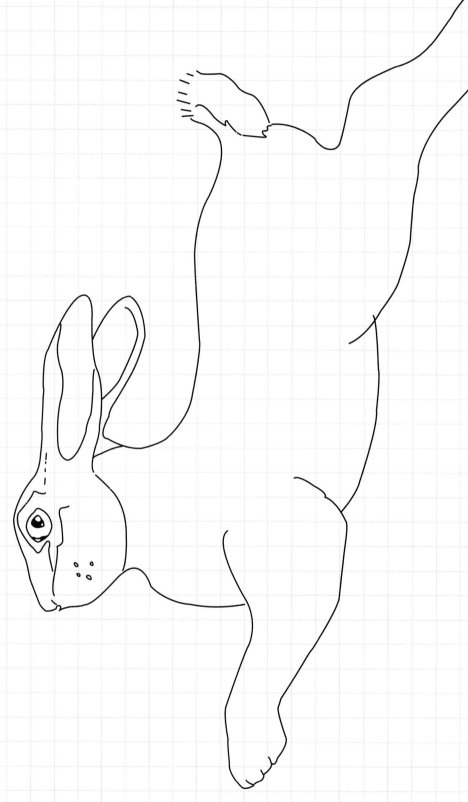

Wild strawberry book cover

Page 154

Glossary

aida cloth

A type of stiffened cotton fabric, specially designed for cross-stitch. The open square weave has regularly spaced holes from 7 to 22 holes per 1 inch (2.5 cm). This is known as the 'count': the smaller the number, the larger the stitches will be.

air-erasable pen

A pen with a special ink that fades away over time; useful for marking outlines and tracing templates.

appliqué

A form of surface decoration in which cutout fabric motifs are stitched onto a background of a second fabric.

basting

Long temporary stitches, worked in a contrasting color, that are used to hold two pieces of fabric together before machine stitching.

batting

A thick, nonwoven fabric sold by length, that is used as the filling in quilted items and as a soft padding.

bias

Fabric cut "on the bias" is cut diagonally, at 45 degrees across the woven threads, making it stretchy.

bias binding

A narrow strip of fabric, cut on the bias, used for binding raw edges. Store-bought bias tape comes with a turning pressed along each side.

bound edge

A fabric edge neatened by folding and stitching a narrow fabric strip over the raw, cut threads.

drawn threadwork

A decorative technique in which horizontal threads are drawn out of the background fabric. The remaining vertical threads are then stitched together in clusters to make a square or triangular lattice.

dressmaker's carbon paper

A thin sheet of paper, coated with a transferable, nonsmudging pigment on one side, used for transferring embroidery outlines onto the background fabric.

evenweave linen

A woven textile in which the warp and weft—the threads that run from top to bottom and side to side—are of equal thickness. It comes in different weights: Sajou's embroidery linen has a count of 32 threads for fine, regular stitches.

fusible interweaving

A fine, heat-activated adhesive with a paper backing that is used to bond two layers of fabric together.

gingham

A yarn-dyed woven fabric with a checked pattern of small light, dark, and mid-toned squares.

guipure lace

A machine-made lace edging with noted, three-dimensional motifs.

interfacing

A nonwoven fabric used to stiffen and reinforce fabric bags and purses. It comes in both iron-on and sew-in versions.

iron-on hemming tape

A narrow strip of fusible adhesive slipped under a turned hem and pressed with a hot iron; a quick alternative to hand sewing a hem.

mitered corner

The point where two hemmed edges meet at a right angle. Each edge is folded back at 45 degrees to make a neat, squared-off junction.

notch

A small V shape cut made into a seam allowance.

openwork

The term for decorative embroidery techniques that create a lacelike pattern of holes in a woven fabric.

piping

A decorative trim used to define the edges of soft furnishings. It consists of a strip of bias-cut fabric that is folded over a fine cord and stitched into the seam line.

flanged piping cord

An upholstery cord with an integral narrow tape used for piping seams.

pleat

A stitched-down double fold that reduces the width of a piece of fabric at one edge and gives fullness to the opposite edge.

pulled threadwork

A type of openwork embroidery in which groups of threads are pulled up tightly together with rows of stitches to make a geometric pattern within the background fabric.

quilter's safety pins

Small angled pins for inserting through several layers of fabric.

rickrack

A flat, narrow woven braid with a wave-like zigzag shape. It comes in a range of widths and colors and is often used on children's clothing.

right side

The finished, printed side of a patterned fabric; the front face of any work in progress.

seam allowance

The two narrow strips of fabric that lie between the stitch line and the outside edge when two pieces of fabric are joined together.

sheeting

A plain white fabric used for bed linen. Use pure cotton sheeting with a thread count of 200 or less for embroidery; it can be difficult to stitch through fine fabric.

ticking

A utilitarian woven striped fabric originally used for pillows and mattress covers.

Tonkin thread

A polyester thread that contains a fine strand of gold lurex for a subtle metallic finish. It was originally produced for haute couture embroiderers and is available in a range of 24 colors.

wrong side

The reverse face of a printed fabric; also the back of any work in progress—the side on which the seam allowances are visible.

Index

Acknowledgments

In England, I would like to thank Lucinda Ganderton who has put all the Sajou products to good use in the lovely projects she has designed for this book, and Sophie Collins for admiring Sajou and coming up with the idea of the book in the first place.

In Paris, warmest thanks are due to my colleague Carolyn Dew, who has translated our work into English from the start and thus gave our website an international angle from the very beginning, and to my daughters, Flavie Deleval, who manages our photography and helps me with the styling of both site and products, and Balsamie Deleval, who manages our brand new Sajou store in the centre of the city.

Frédérique Crestin-Billet

No writer works in isolation, and I am hugely indebted to the creative team at Ivy Press who put this book together. Special thanks to everybody who made it happen: Jacqui Sayers and Jayne Ansell for their editorial skills, support and understanding; Wayne Blades for his faultless design sense; photographer Neal Grundy and stylist Hélène Adamczewski for the inspirational pictures; Cathy Brear for the wonderful illustrations, which add so much to the instructions; Sarah Hoggett for her eagle-eyed text editing; and Sophie Collins for having such faith in me and for inviting me to do the book in the first place. Finally, I am very grateful to Frédérique Crestin-Billet for letting me share her vision. Working on *The Maison Sajou Sewing Book* has been a true delight.

Lucinda Ganderton